WHY CAN'T I ɴᴇʟᴘ THIS
CHILD TO LEARN?

Other titles in the UKCP Series:

WHY CAN'T I HELP THIS CHILD TO LEARN?

Understanding Emotional Barriers to Learning

Edited by

Helen High

On behalf of the United Kingdom Council
for Psychotherapy

KARNAC

Published in 2012 by
Karnac Books Ltd
118 Finchley Road, London NW3 5HT

British Library Cataloguing in Publication Data

A C.I.P. for this book is available from the British Library

ISBN: 978-1-85575-787-5

Edited, designed and produced by Exeter Premedia Services Private Ltd
www.exeterpremedia.com

Printed in Great Britain

www.karnacbooks.com

CONTENTS

CHAPTER TEN

ACKNOWLEDGEMENTS

I wish to express my gratitude: to my husband, Bob High, for his invaluable help with computer knowledge and skills and his patience and tolerance over my reduced availability for other activities while involved in the writing-cum-editing of this book; to Lee Marsden, editor of the Caspari Foundation's journal, for permission to include, as chapters in this book, articles by Jenny Dover and Mia Beaumont previously published as articles in the Caspari Foundation's journal (see below for details); to Kate Barrows for permission to use an example from her article "A Child's Difficulties in Using His Gifts and His Imagination" (Barrows, 1984); to Shirley Hart, Librarian at the British Association of Psychotherapists, for her time and patience in helping me to track down difficult-to-find references; to all the contributors to this book for sharing their experiences of Educational Psychotherapy in their individual chapters and for their input of ideas and encouragement given to me during the process of compiling this book:

Gillian Salmon, Jenny Dover, Mia Beaumont, Heather Geddes, Muriel Barrett, Gill Morton, Marie Delaney

Permissions summary

Barrows, K. (1984). A child's difficulties in using his gifts and his imagination. *Journal of Child Psychotherapy*, 10(1): 15–26.

Beaumont, M. (1988). The effect of loss on learning: the stillborn sibling. *The Journal of Educational Therapy*, 2(1): 33–47.

Dover, J. (2004). Work with a hard-to-reach child. *Educational Therapy & Therapeutic Teaching*, 13: 7–15.

Muriel Barrett is a retired Educational Psychotherapist who was appointed to work as a Remedial Teacher in the Department for Children and Parents, at the Tavistock Clinic, in 1971. Under the influence of Irene Caspari and other members of the multidisciplinary team in that department, she developed the skills that led to her becoming an Educational Psychotherapist. John Bowlby was the Consultant Psychiatrist in the team at that time and it was under his influence that she became interested in the effect of children's attachment patterns on their learning. From 1974 to 1976 she collaborated with Irene Caspari and Consultant Psychiatrist Dr. Dorothy Heard in planning to start training in Educational Therapy at the Tavistock Clinic. This plan did not come to fruition due to Irene Caspari's untimely death in 1976, but Muriel Barrett continued with the planning and set up the first training in Educational Therapy in 1979. She ran workshops on educational therapy in Canada, Holland, the USA, and Norway, which led to the setting up of international conferences and fostered international links with others in this field of work, in particular with educational therapists in Norway. She was strongly influenced by Dorothy Heard in developing an interest in work with families in which a child's learning difficulties were connected with disturbances in family relationships; the topic of the chapter she has contributed to this book. Her earlier work as a teacher spanned the whole age range from primary school to adult education. Reflecting on her teaching career, it occurred to her that she started off with five year olds and ended up with forty-five year olds! She worked in the School Psychological Services for some time before joining the staff of the Tavistock Clinic. She has published articles in journals; is the joint author, with Jane Trevitt, of *Attachment Behaviour and the Schoolchild* (Routledge, 1991); and joint editor, with Ved Varma, of *Educational Therapy in Clinic and Classroom* (Whurr, 1996).

Mia Beaumont currently works in private practice as an Educational Psychotherapist and an Adult Psychotherapist and works with individual children and groups in an inner city primary school. She teaches and supervises trainees on the Caspari Foundation's MA course in Educational Psychotherapy, teaches in the Caspari Foundation's external training courses, and has run whole day events in various locations, including Belfast, Southend, and Hertford. From 1961 to 1978 she worked in various educational settings, including the Polytechnic of North London and secondary, primary, infant, and nursery schools in Islinghton and Hackney, as a language development specialist and a special needs teacher. She trained as an Educational Psychotherapist at the Tavistock Clinic and from 1978 to 1998, she worked in that capacity in a Child and Adolescent Mental Health Service in North London. She was a Joint Organizing Tutor for the training in Educational Therapy from 1986 to 1992 and was Chair of the Caspari Foundation from 2001 to 2006. She trained as an Adult Psychotherapist at the Guild of Psychotherapists. She has published a number of journal articles and chapters for books.

Marie Delaney is Director of The Learning Harbour, Crosshaven, Co. Cork. She trained in the UK as an Educational Psychotherapist, Teacher, and Trainer and has recently relocated to Ireland. She has extensive experience of working with the challenging behaviour— of both staff and pupils! She has worked in projects outside the school system at the Dalston Youth Project, a Mentoring and Education programme in Hackney East London, for young offenders and those at risk of offending, as well as in schools, as a Learning Support Manager, Learning Mentor/Learning Support Co-ordinator for Havering, and as an Emotional Literacy Manager at the Bower Park School, Romford. She is currently working in a school for children with Social, Emotional, and Behaviour Disorders, in Cork, and as a staff trainer. She was also a trainer and moderator in the Department for Education and Science's National Training for Learning Mentors. She has trained teachers in the UK and abroad. Her main interests are introducing therapeutic approaches into mainstream schools, integrating the work of behaviour specialists with classroom teachers, bringing nurture group principles into secondary schools, and developing emotionally literate schools. She is the author of *Teaching the Unteachable* (Worth, 2009) and *"What can I do with the kid who?"* (Worth, 2010).

Jenny Dover works as an Educational Psychotherapist in a Child and Adolescent Mental Health Service in an Inner London borough, and has done so for the past twenty-three years. In addition she teaches and supervises trainees on the MA course in Educational Psychotherapy at the Caspari Foundation. She also offers training to educators on the subject of children's emotional development. Previously she taught English literature and became a Special Educational Needs Coordinator before training at the Tavistock Clinic as an Educational Psychotherapist. From 2004 onwards she has published a number of journal articles on Educational Therapy/Psychotherapy, has written a chapter for a book on Educational Therapy and is the joint author, with Gillian Salmon, of the book, *Reaching and Teaching Through Educational Psychotherapy: A Case Study Approach*, published in 2007.

Dr Heather Geddes is an Educational Psychotherapist. She began teaching in 1974 in the Science Department of a large girls' comprehensive school and soon became interested in the pupils who seemed unable to access learning. She went on to become Teacher-in-Charge in a social services Intermediate Treatment Unit, working with young people who were outside the school system and socially at risk. While working in that role she attended an evening course at the Tavistock Clinic on Psychological Aspects of Learning Difficulties. She has since worked in a variety of settings in Education and in Child and Adolescent Mental Health Services, concerned primarily with pupils presenting with challenging behaviours. Her particular interests are the social, emotional, and behaviour difficulties that inhibit learning. She has undertaken relevant research on how to help teachers to work effectively with such children, and in particular, on the links between Attachment and Learning, which was the subject of her thesis for a PhD at Roehampton University. She currently works as a supervisor, trainer, and consultant, with links to services for Looked After Children and Fostering and Adoption. She has taught and supervised trainees of the Caspari Foundation's MA Course in Educational Psychotherapy, has published many journal articles and chapters in books, was co-editor of a Special Issue of the *Journal of Psychodynamic Practice*, in 2002, and is the author of the book, *Attachment in the Classroom* (Worth, 2006).

Helen High is an Educational Psychotherapist and a Child and Adult Psychotherapist. Having retired from work in the National Health Service (NHS) she currently sees a small number of adult patients in private practice. She teaches and serves on the Training Committee of the Child and Adolescent Psychotherapy Training, at the British Association for Psychotherapists. She is a founder member of the Caspari Foundation, was the Joint Organizing Tutor/ Programme Convenor of the Training in Educational Therapy from 1986 to 1998 and takes an active part in planning and teaching on the Masters (MA) course of training in Educational Psychotherapy. She worked as an Infants teacher for three years before training as an Educational Psychologist at the Tavistock Clinic, where, as part of that training, Irene Caspari supervised her on individual and small group work with children who had specific learning difficulties in reading, and subsequently involved her in teaching and becoming an Organizing Tutor of an evening course for teachers on the "Psychological Aspects of Learning Difficulties", the course that laid the foundation for the development of the Caspari Foundation. Having worked as an Educational Psychologist for thirteen years she returned to the Tavistock Clinic to train as a Child Psychotherapist. While undertaking that training she also worked there, part-time, as a Psychologist and Tutor for Educational Psychology Training. On completion of that training she worked for seventeen years as a part-time Child Psychotherapist in the NHS Clinics, while continuing her involvement in Educational Psychotherapy training. She trained as an Adult Psychotherapist at the British Association of Psychotherapists (BAP) in the 1990s, with a view to working privately in semi-retirement. She has published a number of journal articles and contributed chapters to books.

Gill Morton is an Educational Psychotherapist who has specialized in running Therapeutic Story Groups in mainstream schools and in training others in this work by involving a school staff member in working alongside her when she runs such a group. She began work as a primary school teacher in Birmingham and London. Moving from class teaching to second language teaching, she developed an interest in behaviour in groups. She went on to work in Nurture Groups for young children, who seemed unready for school. Seeking help to understand their complex difficulties, she undertook Educational Therapy training at the Tavistock Clinic. Since then, she has moved through a number of different work settings, working as:

- a peripatetic teacher for the Inner London Authority School Psychological Service
- an Educational Therapist in a Child and Family Consultation Service
- a teacher of small groups at the Tavistock Day Unit
- a member of a team working with families in the Education Unit of the Marlborough Family Service

In exploring the different demands of the work in these varied contexts, she became increasingly interested in how children can make use of therapeutic story groups, particularly within mainstream school settings. She teaches on the Caspari Foundation courses, including the MA course of training in Educational Psychotherapy, for which she has also supervised trainees. She has contributed to a Therapeutic Story Group project in a North East London borough and to the Masters course in Educational Therapy at the University of Trondheim, Norway. She has published journal articles and chapters in books.

Gillian Salmon now works in private practice as a Consultant Educational Psychologist and Educational Psychotherapist, offering assessment of the learning needs of children and adolescents and supervision of the work of Educational Psychotherapists. She worked as a teacher in a variety of schools before training as an Educational Psychotherapist at the Tavistock Clinic. She later trained as an Educational Psychologist at Edinburgh University and worked in this role with the Local Education Authorities in Bromley and Essex. She was, from 1992 to 2004, the Joint Organizing Tutor, and then Programme Leader, of the MA in Educational Psychotherapy at the Caspari Foundation and is currently Chair of the Caspari Foundation's Governing Board. She has published a number of journal articles and chapters in books on Educational Psychotherapy during the 1990s and is the joint author, with Jenny Dover, of the book, *Reaching and Teaching Through Educational Psychotherapy: A Case Study Approach*, published in 2007 (Wiley).

Introduction: the origins of educational psychotherapy

Helen High

Educational Psychotherapy combines direct teaching and an indirect therapeutic method of working with underlying emotional problems that act as barriers to learning.

In London, this approach was pioneered by Irene Caspari at the Tavistock Clinic, while she was a member of the psychology staff, in the Clinic's Department for Children and Parents, from the 1950s to 1976. She had been a teacher for many years, before training as a psychologist, and was puzzled by some of the children and adolescents referred to the Clinic, who had specific difficulties in learning to read. These included children of average or above-average intelligence, who showed no sign of the kind of difficulty in discriminating between similar shapes that hamper children in recognizing words and letters. What was stopping these children learning to read? There was no obvious cause for their failure.

Caspari set about studying the problems of these puzzling children and found that they often became acutely anxious and/or resistant to learning when faced with the specific kind of learning task with which they had difficulty. She came to understand that their emotional problems were interfering with their learning. To address these problems, Caspari started to work with individual children who had specific reading difficulties, seeing them for regular individual sessions once a week or more. In these sessions she spent part of the time presenting the child with a task related to the child's specific area of learning difficulty and the rest of the time in activities that offered an opportunity for self-expression, such as drawing, painting, play, or making up stories.

While developing her understanding of emotional problems that interfered with learning, Caspari continued to draw on, and apply, theoretical principles derived from her training and experience as a teacher and educational psychologist. She also learnt from her psychiatric and psychotherapeutically trained colleagues in the Clinic's multidisciplinary team, and from reading professional literature on the subject, about the psychoanalytic findings regarding emotional conflicts that inhibit some children's learning. During her time at the Tavistock Clinic she developed a therapeutic approach to working with such children, now known as Educational Psychotherapy.

It is specific to Educational Psychotherapy, as opposed to Child Psychotherapy, that the child's or adolescent's learning difficulties and emotional problems are being addressed by the same person, within the same relationship. If, during an Educational Psychotherapy session, a child's anxiety is stirred up by a particular learning activity, the therapist may suggest a change of activity at that specific moment. Offering the child or adolescent an opportunity for self-expression, through activities such as play, drawing, or making up a story, at the very point when the anxiety has been aroused by the learning task, tends to prompt an expression of the underlying anxiety. This gives an immediate and safe outlet for the expression of the anxiety, which relieves the child from the stress of keeping it bottled up and opens up a way of talking about it with the same person who is in the teaching role. For example, Peter, a nine-year old, who could hardly read at all, often became acutely anxious while reading in his Educational Psychotherapy sessions with me. I would stop him when the anxiety mounted beyond a certain stage and suggest that he chose what to do next. Typically he would draw, or make paper aeroplanes, depicting scenes of the planes crashing and burning. He would scribble furiously on the paper planes using red pencil to represent the flames. This gave an indirect expression to the feelings and fantasies that had become linked with reading in his mind, and gave us an opportunity to explore the underlying meaning of these feelings. I talked to him about the dangerous things happening in his play and drawings and linked them with his fear that his angry and destructive feelings could be dangerous. These emotions had become linked in his unconscious mind with the activity of reading. Working in this way with his emotional problems, along with teaching him in a way that gave him confidence in his ability to learn to read, helped us, over time, to disentangle his emotional problems from his learning (see Chapter One).

It was not until after Caspari's death, in 1976, that it came to light that, at the Nic Waals Psychiatric Clinic in Oslo, Anne Marit Sletten Duve who, like Irene Caspari, was an experienced teacher before joining the multidisciplinary staff of a Child Psychiatric Clinic, had independently developed a very similar method of treating such children. On learning about Anne Marit's work, I felt sad that these two pioneers of Educational Psychotherapy had not had the opportunity to meet and compare notes about their experience and methods of working. However, the fact that, with similar backgrounds of professional experience, they independently made similar discoveries about such children's problems and developed similar ways of working with them does serve to validate Educational Psychotherapy's professional contribution (Sletten Duve, 1988).

PART I

THE THEORETICAL BACKGROUND
TO EDUCATIONAL PSYCHOTHERAPY

CHAPTER ONE

Theoretical principles applied in educational psychotherapy

Helen High

In developing the theory and practice of Educational Psychotherapy, Irene Caspari drew on a variety of theoretical principles derived from the study of:

A. Cognitive Development and Behavioural Theory
B. Attachment Theory
C. Psychoanalytic Theories of Child Development and Defence Mechanisms (see Chapter Two).

Cognitive development and behavioural theory

In her thinking about teaching children who have specific difficulties in learning, the following principles were central to Irene Caspari's thinking:

1. Practice is essential to master a skill.
2. The motivation to master a skill can bring its own reward when the person experiences sufficient improvement with practice to enjoy the feeling of progressively mastering that skill.

3.   Those who have difficulty in learning a skill need more practice than others, which can be irksome and discouraging.

4.   When there has been a history of failure in learning, the main motivation may be to avoid the pain of further failure by avoiding tasks associated with that failure.

Caspari concluded that it was essential to tackle the demoralization of children who had developed an aversion to learning through a history of failure. She did so by breaking the learning task into small easy steps, to ensure sufficient experience of success at each step. This thinking was in line with Behaviour Modification principles based on the Learning Theory of conditioning by means of rewards and punishments.

Case example

On testing Peter, the nine-year-old boy I referred to in the Introduction, he proved to be of average intelligence and showed no evidence of any specific cognitive or perceptual problem. He was almost a complete non-reader when I started seeing him once a week for educational psychotherapy. He was extremely resistant to any reading task, particularly reading from books, and became very anxious when attempting to read. In order to introduce Peter to a reading task in small steps, I dispensed with books for the time being and used very simple word and picture matching cards. I helped him to match nine 3-letter words to pictures of the objects named on the cards, before asking him to do so on his own. He could only match two or three of the nine words to the right pictures. I helped him with the others, encouraging him to try to memorize them. Over several weeks, with repeated practice, he gradually learnt the rest of them until one week he got them all right. I then suggested that, as he now knew all those words, he might like to try the next set of cards. He said "No, I want to do that one again". In fact he did it over and over again, as if to get his fill of this experience of perfect success. I am sure it was a first for him to manage to complete a reading task without a single mistake. This was a turning point for Peter. The experience of finding that he could learn words he had not known before and perform a task perfectly, convinced him that he was capable of learning to read. This made a huge difference to his motivation. There was a lot more to his resistant attitude to reading than that, as will be described later (see pp. 25–26), but his tendency to give up and avoid the painful experience of failure was an important element in his resistance. Giving him tasks that were easy enough to enable him to experience success overcame that element. It was then possible to introduce new learning very gradually and help him with it while he continued to experience more success than failure at each stage on the way. When he had built up a sufficient sight vocabulary, and had learnt to sound out simple new words phonetically, we went back to reading books. I chose a series of books in which the vocabulary was carefully graded so that new words were introduced slowly and used repeatedly to reinforce learning. He was delighted to discover that he could now read books. With children like Peter, who are so discouraged and turned off from learning by their history of failure, it is very important to find a level at which they can feel rewarded by the experience of success.

Attachment theory

Caspari's colleagues at the Tavistock Clinic included John Bowlby. His research collaborators included Mary Ainsworth, who helped to identify patterns of attachment that first develop during infancy.

The secure attachment pattern

When mothers were sufficiently attuned and responsive to their babies' needs in early infancy, the babies became securely attached to their mothers. As long as they experienced their mothers as reliably there to return to, securely attached infants felt safe to explore, to reach out to the wider world, to learn about it and the objects in it.

The anxious-ambivalent attachment pattern

When a mother's behaviour towards her baby was inconsistent and unpredictable the infant developed an anxious-ambivalent attachment pattern.

The anxious-avoidant behaviour pattern

When a mother was rejecting in her responses to her baby an anxious-avoidant behaviour pattern ensued.

These attachment patterns, first developed during infancy, persist into later life, and are transferred into later relationships, including relationships with teachers. While a child with a secure attachment pattern will tend to be ready to trust his/her teacher, an insecure attachment pattern interferes with the development of trust. Learning in school takes place in a relationship between child and teacher, so whatever attitudes, expectations, hopes, or fears the child brings to that learning relationship affects the child's capacity to learn from the teacher.

The disorganized/disorientated attachment pattern

Some babies showed disorganized/disorientated behaviour in the mother's presence during the research study, freezing with a trance-like expression hands-in-air, or turning away from the mother to the wall while crying.

These peculiar behaviours were concluded by Main and her colleagues to show a disorganized version of one of the three typical patterns, most commonly the anxious-resistant pattern (Main & Weston, 1981). Some infants who showed these aberrant patterns of behaviour had been physically abused or neglected by the parent. Others had mothers who had themselves been abused as children, or were still preoccupied with mourning the loss of a parent during their childhood, or who were suffering from a severe manic depressive illness and were very unpredictable in the treatment of their child.

Case example

In a previous article Jenny Dover described a child with an anxious-ambivalent attachment pattern, who was referred to the Child and Adolescent Mental Health Services (CAMHS) by her teacher. The teacher described her as, "In my face constantly and very demanding of my attention, but cannot settle to a task although she is intelligent. She seems terribly unhappy and I fear she gets nothing out of school". In the early stages of Educational Psychotherapy, Dover found, "While Carla rejects me as a teacher, her behaviour is designed to keep my attention constantly on her so that our interaction, though negative, is ceaseless. She cannot disconnect from me sufficiently to focus on a task" (Dover, 2003).

In Chapter Five, on "Work with a Hard-to-Reach Child", Jenny Dover gives an example of a child whose avoidant attachment pattern was a strong barrier to being taught, as he avoided contact with her and did not let her know when he needed help. The chapter illustrates how an indirect approach, which allowed this avoidant child to express his emotional problems, related to his traumatic family experience through the medium of a serial story, which had a therapeutic effect and led to progress in his learning.

CHAPTER TWO

Psychoanalytic theory of development and unconscious mental processes

Helen High

Unconscious mental processes and defence mechanisms

Freud and his colleague Breuer, who were both medical doctors, discovered that when patients whose physical symptoms had no physical cause were asked to talk freely, saying whatever came into their minds, their physical symptoms sometimes cleared up, as they remembered distressing experiences from the past. One of Breuer's patients referred to this as "the talking cure". This led to the discovery of unconscious mental processes and the recovery of memories from the past, which had been repressed, or pushed out of consciousness. Freud concluded that those memories live on some-where in our minds and continue to influence us in ways of which we are unaware. He discovered that they sometimes find expression in disguised ways such as conversion into physical symptoms, as in the patient who referred to "the talking cure".

Case illustration

A 13-year-old boy, Jonathan, had developed paralysis of his right arm (he was right-handed). Medical investigations failed to

---

reveal any physical cause for this symptom. The doctors concerned arranged some physiotherapy for him, but thought that psychological causes should also be investigated. When Jonathan was interviewed to explore the psychological aspects of his problems, he spoke in very disapproving terms of the violent and destructive behaviour of teenagers "these days", commenting, "I'd never do anything like that". After a pause he added, "unless my Dad hit me, then I'd hit him back". He then sat staring silently at his paralysed arm, with which he was powerless to hit anybody.

Freud's formulation about what he called a "conversion symptom", where a physical symptom is related to a psychological problem, was that it expressed, in a disguised form, both sides of an unconscious conflict. Considering his symptom in those terms, Jonathan's paralysed arm can be seen as expressing both his aggressive feelings towards his father, the wish to hit his father, and the wish to stop himself from doing so, by renouncing any aggression ("I'd never do anything like that"). He could not even allow himself a *fantasy* of an aggressive act towards his father, unless he could justify this by imagining his father having hit him first. The psychoanalytic view of a conversion symptom is that the two opposing sides of the conflict neutralize each other in the physical symptom. As a result of this neutralization Jonathan could not do anything with his right arm, he was paralysed. Neither Jonathan nor his parents wanted to think of psychological reasons for his physical symptom and they declined the offer of psychotherapeutic help. As he was showing some improvement since starting physiotherapy, they wanted to carry on with that treatment, hoping it would be enough to help him get over the problem. They did not want anything more to do with the psychological services, so I do not know the outcome. My speculation was that if the symptom of paralysis of his arm cleared up it might be replaced by some other manifestation of the underlying emotional conflict, as is prone to happen with this kind of symptom, if the underlying cause is not resolved.

As Freud was a doctor in the first place, he saw patients with physical complaints and encountered those whose physical symptoms were an indirect expression of psychological problems, as I did in this particular case, which was referred by a doctor. In working with educational problems, however, we more often come across those whose psychological problems are expressed in an attitude to school or a difficulty in learning.

Case illustration

George, a 12-year-old boy I was seeing for educational psychotherapy, became obsessed at one point with the wish to move to another school. He was complaining that everyone at his school was against him, the other children were unkind to him, and none of the teachers liked him. I could not take this at face value, as he had previously talked positively about friends at school. I had also visited his school and met teachers who spoke positively about him and wanted to try to help him. I was sure there was more to it than he was telling me, but I got nowhere in trying to explore things further by direct discussion. When, instead, I suggested he did a drawing, he drew a court scene in which a policeman was dragging him into the dock by the hair in front of an audience of angry-faced onlookers. I imagined the onlookers represented the people at school he was complaining of, but when asked about it he said they were "all my family, angry because I can't read". This gave us the chance to talk about his reading difficulty and his worry about what other members of his family felt about it. After that I heard no more about his wish to change schools. His anxiety about the feelings of "all his family" had been displaced onto "all the people at school". This example illustrates how offering another means of expression for an emotional problem, in this case through a drawing, can enable a child to show more about the underlying problem.

Psychoanalytic theory of stages of child development

Freud developed the theory, based on his experience of psychoanalytic work, that the emotional development of the infant and child is closely related to their experience of bodily functions. He deduced that, from infancy onwards, there are childhood stages of sexual development, in which parts of the body are invested with special qualities of excitability and sensuality, with corresponding emotions and fantasies. He named these stages the Oral Stage, Anal Stage, and Oedipal Stage. The characteristics of these stages are as follows:

The oral stage

Babies begin life with a special sensitivity and sensuality of the mouth. During feeding, pleasurable feelings in the mouth, tongue, and lips are experienced while sucking the nipple of the breast or the teat of the bottle. A baby also explores new objects by putting them in the mouth, learning how they feel by oral sensations, as well as through other senses such as sight and hearing. The baby's relationship with the mother, too, is experienced via the mouth, as a relationship with the breast, or the bottle, is felt to be part of the mother. Needs and emotions are also expressed through the mouth by crying and other vocal utterances. Young children feel and express their emotions very much through their bodies. Their loves and hates are often expressed by the mouth, or experienced as belonging to the activities of the mouth. Nursery age children often express their anger in terms of biting, spitting or such like, either in action or in words. Grown-ups too sometimes say things like "I love her so much I could eat her up". This cannibalistic desire probably starts with the baby at the breast wishing to devour the breast. It expresses a love of total possession.

Some learning difficulties relate to early oral conflicts. Reading, in particular, seems to be equated in our minds with feeding. Like feeding, reading involves taking things in. This is reflected in our language, in the metaphors commonly applied to reading, such as calling someone a voracious reader or a bookworm (Strachey, 1930).

Case illustration

I was asked to see Alan when he was nearly seven years old, because, although intelligent, he was not learning to read. At a few weeks old he had had an operation for a painful condition of the stomach, which obstructed the flow of milk and led to an alarming symptom of violent vomiting. Although the operation had been completely successful, in the subsequent years, Alan's mother continued to be very anxious about Alan's feeding, worrying about whether he was getting enough to eat. This meant his experience of feeding and eating had continued to be imbued with his mother's anxiety. Alan showed signs of emotional disturbance and I thought it likely that his reading difficulty was linked with emotional problems. He was placed in a small class, with an experienced Infants Teacher, in a special unit for children with emotional and behaviour difficulties. When he could not spell a word, he would ask the teacher to write it on a piece of paper for him to copy into his written work. The teacher began to notice that, after copying a word in this way, Alan would habitually put the slip of paper with the word on it into his mouth and chew it. It was as if he was eating the words she had "fed" to him. He made good progress and quite quickly caught up enough to return to mainstream school.

The anal stage

The anal stage relates to toilet training. Before reaching that stage, the mother simply disposes of the baby's dirty nappies, the baby just evacuates. During the toddler stage the child develops sensitivity to bodily sensations, around the anus, that signal the need to evacuate, and gradually learns to control the excretory functions. This control enables the child to give something to, or withhold it from, the mother or carer, who is encouraging the toddler to use business in the potty. In the feeding relationship the mother offers the food and the child can accept or refuse it. In toilet training it is the other way round; the mother wants something from the child, who has some power to give or withhold it. A child's fantasies about its faeces may be of something precious it has produced and does not want to lose. The child may then resent the mother for taking them away and tipping them down the toilet, leaving him/her feeling empty and depleted. Other fantasies that children express are of faeces used as a means of attack, in which case soiling can be a hostile act. Evacuation of the faeces is sometimes experienced in fantasy as an explosive attack.

Case illustration

I was seeing Roger for Educational Psychotherapy. He was seven years old, of average intelligence, but had a reading difficulty. His father had died two years ago, crushed to death in a tragic accident, in the course of his work. In one of Roger's sessions with me, he was mixing paints. He had a large sheet of paper attached to a small easel. He mixed several different colours of paint in a small plastic pot of water so that the contents ended up as muddy brown in colour. He then took some plasticine, moulded it into several small cup-shaped objects, poured dirty brown paint water into each of these and, sealing up the tops of them, said they were paint bombs. He threw them, one at a time, at the sheet of paper on the painting easel. He then took a bigger piece of plasticine, with which he sealed the top of the plastic pot containing the rest of the paint water, and threw it at the easel. The brown paint water ran down the paper in a smeary mess. Roger then went over to the easel and, with his finger, traced in the brown wet paint mixture the letters s-h-i-t. I read the word out loud saying " 'Shit'-, oh that's what it is, is it?" He said "Yes" in emphatic tones. I added "and I think you want me to clear it all up, just like a Mummy clearing up a baby's nappy". He replied "Yes, *just* like that!" Following this he drew two stick-figures, clearly representing the two of us since one of the figures had his initial, R, above its head and the other H, the initial of my surname. There was a vertical line, representing the side view of the paint easel, and a series of circular shapes in an arc, representing the paint bombs flying through the air. I was behind the easel. One of the paint bombs was shown as hitting the easel, while another was going over the top of the easel and hitting me! This was clearly a fantasy of an anal attack on me.

The genital stage and the Oedipus Complex

At the age of about three to five years, children's genital organs become the focus of sensual sensitivity and interest. Sometimes children feel stimulated in the genital region while being washed and obtain pleasure from that. In the case study of four-year-old "Little Hans", whose father had sought Freud's advice about the child, Freud describes an incident the father reported to him when Hans was four-and-a-quarter. While the mother had been drying and powdering Hans after a bath, and taking care not to touch his penis as she powdered around it, Hans had asked her why she didn't put her finger there. He responded to his mother's replies that it would be "piggish" and "not proper" by laughing and saying "But it's great fun". At this stage children normally become aware of the differences between boys' and girls' bodies and very interested in and curious about where babies come from and how they are made. Along with this they become acutely aware of relationships between members of their own family, including the parents' relationship with each other. Freud used the term "Oedipus Complex" for this phase of development, which also involves rivalry with the parent of the same sex in relation to the parent of the opposite sex; the child having a fantasy of ousting the rival parent and taking over as Mummy's or Daddy's husband or wife.

Case illustration 1

Five-year-old Tony stayed with his grandparents for a weekend, two or three months after his baby brother was born. While there, he decided to draw a picture of the family to take home for his mother. He drew the family members in a line, first Mummy, then himself, then the baby, then Daddy. He then showed the drawing to his grandmother, and pointing to Daddy said, "Daddy's cross because Mummy and I love each other". He had placed himself closest to his mother—between her and the new baby—and his father furthest away from his mother. This seemed a clear expression of his Oedipal wish to be closest to his Mummy, and the main love of her life, so that his father would feel angry about being excluded from that special relationship with his mother instead of him having to bear the feelings of exclusion, anger, and jealousy. Attributing those feelings to his father was his way of protecting himself from *his* feelings of exclusion from the parents' relationship with each other and with the new baby, at a time when he would have been at the height of the Oedipal stage of development.

Case illustration 2

Caspari gave an example of a 10-year-old boy who could not synthesize the letter sounds when attempting to read three-letter words. In talking about three-letter words he said that the first letter was the father, the last letter the mother and the letter in the middle the child. Caspari wrote

> His mother reported that he insisted on watching television at night from his bed. This was only possible if the door between his bedroom and their sitting room was left open and the parents put their chairs on either side of the door. In this way, the familiar pattern of the child coming between the parents, in the three person situation in the family, was repeatedly enacted in the home, and the inability to analyse and synthesise three letter words seemed to be directly related to this situation. [Caspari, 1986, p. 40]

Freud described the child as normally emerging from this phase at the age of about seven and accepting the reality of the parents' relationship with each other. The acceptance of the reality that the daydream of marrying Mummy or Daddy will not come true is both disillusioning and reassuring to the child. On reaching this stage satisfactorily, a child settles for identifying with, and aiming to be like the parent of the same sex and accepts the need to wait to grow up to have its own partner. Along with this there is a turning away from the intensity of sexual interest in one parent, and the conflict between love and hate towards the rivalled parent. This brings relief from the conflict, confusion, and anxiety of the intense mixed feelings of the Oedipal stage, which tend to lie dormant during the next phase.

The latency stage

Between the Oedipal stage and the onset of puberty, sexual impulses and preoccupations are normally less prominent. They tend to be put on hold, until the maturing of the sexual organs, and accompanying hormonal changes of puberty and adolescence stir them up powerfully. In turning away from those preoccupations the child turns more towards an interest in the outside world and learning about it and towards friendships with other children. This stage is a fruitful one for education, in which children tend to be motivated to learn, less distracted by inner emotional pressures, and more able to respond to what school has to offer. When, however, a child has unresolved conflicts belonging to an earlier stage, this can interfere with learning, as in Caspari's example of the 10-year-old boy, whose inability to synthesize three letter words was related to his Oedipal wish to come between his parents.

Puberty and adolescence

The latency phase ends with the onset of puberty. In the process of growing from child to adult, the adolescent has to come to terms with a changing body and a changing identity. There is rapid growth along with maturing of sexual organs, with accompanying hormonal changes and an upsurge of sexual impulses and emotions. Emotionally it is a turbulent time. It can be exciting, full of interesting new possibilities, but also overwhelming and confusing. These developmental changes bring challenges and anxieties for the adolescents themselves, and for parents and teachers, about the adolescents' control of both sexual and aggressive impulses. It is obvious that lack of control in adolescents, who grow to be as big and strong as adults, can be dangerous. Unresolved conflicts and anxieties from earlier stages tend to get stirred up again at the onset of adolescence and complicate the emergence of adolescent sexuality. For example, when a girl first starts her periods she may feel disgust at finding a bloodstain on her knickers, and embarrassment at being incontinent, in spite of being well-informed about menstruation, because it stirs up feelings about lack of control of bodily functions, deriving from the anal stage. Dormant Oedipal sexual feelings and fantasies may also be stirred up again and confused with the emerging adolescent sexuality. However, the resurgence of these earlier conflicts in adolescence gives a second chance to work them over again, with the possibility of reaching a better resolution. The adolescent has the task of moving away from childhood dependence and Oedipal ties to parents, towards adult independence and mature relationships, including sexual relationships.

Learning difficulties in adolescence

The skills of reading, writing, and numeracy are of crucial importance for leading an independent adult life. For example, the ability to read street names is crucial in order to find your own way around in an unfamiliar place. An adolescent, who has a long-standing learning difficulty in any of these basic skills, has usually, by that time of life, become discouraged by failure and may try to hide the difficulty. While giving a reading test to a teenage boy of above average intelligence with a reading difficulty, I noticed that while he was reading a continuous passage, if he encountered a word he found difficult to read he guessed it from the context. This worked a lot of the time, but sometimes he guessed wrongly and misunderstood the meaning of what he was reading. When reading individual words out of context his level of success was much lower as he had no context to help him guess. When I asked him how he got on with written work in school, he talked of difficulty in remembering how to spell longer words. If he could not spell a word, he tried to think of another way to put what he wanted to say, using words that were easier to spell. This covered up his difficulty in spelling to some extent, but meant he avoided learning to spell new words or letting the teacher know when he needed help to do so. The use of these evasive tactics was a clever way to work round his problems, but it held back his progress in spelling. The trouble is that a teenager who cannot read or spell feels humiliated by appearing so childish. In working with adolescents with such problems it is helpful to talk to them in an adult way about their difficulties in order to respect their level of maturity and to try to enlist the relatively mature side of the young person in understanding and tackling their difficulties.

Defence mechanisms

Freud identified ways in which people protect themselves from anxieties, emotions, or emotional conflicts, which feel unacceptable, overwhelming or too painful to bear. He called these defence mechanisms. The following are examples of defence mechanisms that help or hinder learning:

Identification

Identifying with and wishing to emulate a teacher who is enthusiastic about learning can enhance a child's motivation to learn.

Identification with the aggressor

The defence mechanism that operates in a bullying behaviour, however, is a destructive force within the educational system. The defence against feeling frightened is to frighten someone else by identifying with and becoming a frightening figure. This also involves projection.

Projection

Projection is the attribution of ones own feelings to others. Bullies, for example, may project frightened feelings into their victims to defend themselves from feeling frightened.

Denial

Denial is the sense of denying feelings one cannot consciously admit to oneself. In denial the feeling is repressed, as in a child threatened with violence by another who convinces himself "I'm not scared".

Splitting

Children may protect themselves from the conflict and anxiety of having ambivalent feelings, such as mixed feelings of love and hate for the same person, by trying to keep the opposing feelings apart. In their inner worlds they direct their love and their hate towards different people, idealizing the loved one(s) and denigrating the hated one(s). In this state of mind they tend to see other people as either good or bad, splitting these opposing feelings apart to avoid emotional confusion and conflict. This can occur in relation to teachers in the Secondary School setting where a pupil is taught by a number of different teachers. One teacher may be adored and idealized, for example, in a typical teenage crush, but this is often at the expense of another teacher who is hated, despised, and denigrated. If the teachers involved realize this is happening, they may be able to avoid colluding with the roles they are cast in. This defence against ambivalent feelings protects the individual from the anxiety that their anger and hatred may be more powerful than their love and may damage those they care about. Splitting their good and bad feelings apart goes along with projecting their affectionate and caring feelings onto some people and their hostility onto others. The penalty for this is that "the others" are then experienced as hostile and threatening.

Case illustration

Gerald, who had felt abandoned at the age of seven when his mother suddenly left home, often missed one or more of his Educational Psychotherapy sessions following a holiday break. I discussed this with him after such a missed session when he was 12 years old. He said he was scared coming on the bus on his own. He was frightened of people on the bus, imagining they were laughing at him and might want him to go with them. This sounded like a fear of being kidnapped. This anxiety only came up when I had not been available to him during a holiday time. It seemed he then experienced me like an abandoning mother. He was undoubtedly angry with his mother for abandoning him, and with me for not being there for him in the holidays. It seems that he split off his angry feelings to preserve his good feelings towards his mother and me, and projected them into other people whom he then perceived as hostile. He then felt frightened of those people and thought they were out to get him.

Sublimation

Sublimation is a defence that helps learning, in which instinctual drives are channelled into socially acceptable activities. An obvious example is aggression channelled into sporting activity. Somewhat more subtle is the channelling of aggression into academic learning. Sublimated aggression can be harnessed to provide the mental energy needed to "tackle" or "battle" with a difficult task, to "get one's teeth into it" or to "grapple" or "struggle" with the problem, to quote a few of the aggressive metaphors commonly used in such a context.

A book by Anna Freud, daughter of Sigmund Freud and a pioneer of Child Psychoanalysis, gives a detailed account of the mechanisms of defence, with illustrative examples (Freud, 1937, reprinted 1986).

Confusion of fantasy and reality

Melanie Klein, the other pioneer of Child Psychoanalysis, wrote about anxieties and fantasies, which in some cases, become linked with a specific learning activity, such as, learning to read or write. This happens when confusion between fantasy and reality leads to confusion between the symbol and the object symbolized.

Case illustration

Kate Barrows, a Child Psychotherapist, describes a seven-year-old boy, Leroy, whom she encountered early in her career when working as a play leader in an Adventure Playground (Barrows, 1984). She was asked to try to help Leroy learn to read. She noticed that when faced with a reading book, he looked scared. She told him she thought he looked frightened. In response, he pointed to certain letters on the page saying they were animals, lions, and tigers with sharp teeth. He looked as if he expected the words to leap off the page and bite him. When Barrows encouraged him to go on talking he spoke anxiously about bad fights his parents had and how scared he felt when they fought. In the course of a few more sessions of half-an-hour or so, in which Leroy talked about his anxieties, with Barrows as an attentive listener, his reading progressed markedly. The letters on the page were not merely symbolic of the teeth of lions and tigers for that child, they were literally felt to *be* those dangerous teeth and reading was felt to be fraught with danger. Leroy's anxieties about the fights between his parents were projected onto the symbols for letters and words. He then felt the words were dangerous and to be avoided, which interfered with his progress in reading. When given the opportunity to express his anxieties to a receptive listener, in a way that felt safe, he could accept direct help with his reading from the person who had noticed his anxiety and listened sympathetically to what it was about. He responded quickly and readily to this timely intervention. Sometimes, emotional problems are more complicated and entrenched, deeply defended against, and difficult to access, in which case psychotherapeutic help may be needed.

In an article on "A contribution to the Theory of Intellectual Inhibition", Klein wrote about a young boy whose psychoanalysis revealed his repressed fears that his jealous fantasies about potential siblings, not yet born, would actually harm his mother. These fantasies had become associated in his mind with certain

French words that he confused with each other, which interfered with his learning French (Klein, 1931, 1975). In such cases, the child fears that their inner hostile fantasies can actually harm a real person in the external world. This confusion between fantasy and reality is prone to affect the learning of symbolic activities such as reading, writing, and mathematics.

In Chapter Six on "The Effect of Loss on Learning: The Stillborn Sibling", Mia Beaumont draws on Melanie Klein's article on this subject, in writing about the educational psychotherapy of a young girl whose mother had failed to mourn the death of an earlier stillborn baby.

Chapter Four, by Gillian Salmon is about the symbolic meaning of fairy tales and their use in Educational Psychotherapy. In it she refers to Bruno Bettelheim's ideas about the emotional significance of fairy and folk tales that have been handed down from generation to generation over many years, becoming part of a cultural tradition (Bettelheim, 1976).

Chapter Seven by Heather Geddes: "A Boy who Used Numbers as a Defence Against Feelings" gives an account of Educational Psychotherapy with a seven-to-eight-year-old boy who was resistant to reading and writing in school and over-reacted to slight triggers by violent outbursts in class and in the playground. He had been traumatized by a history of domestic violence and rejection by his mother. He took to playing competitive games with his therapist, expressing his aggression through the game, and taking responsibility for keeping the scores. He did so particularly at times when he felt rejected by his therapist because she would be unavailable for him, for example, just before a holiday; resorting to numbers as things he felt were safe in order to avoid painful feelings of rejection, like those he felt towards his mother. Later he responded positively to an understanding teacher giving him responsibility for recording number information for her and the class. In discussing this child's problems, Geddes draws on Bion's "Theory of Thinking", in relation to containing the child's emotions (Bion, 1962b), and on the work of Perry et al., on the effects of early traumatic experiences on the development of the brain.

Bion's theory of thinking

In "A Theory of Thinking", Bion suggests that a young baby projects primitive anxieties, such as, the fear of dying, onto the mother (Bion, 1962b). He describes a receptive mother as taking in and containing these projections, working them over in her reverie, imagining what the baby feels, and after processing the infant's fears in this way, handing them back in a thought-about, more benign and bearable form. A baby who repeatedly has the experience of being thought about like this takes in that experience of a thinking, understanding mother, who can contain anxieties and calm the baby's fears. Bion suggests that internalizing such a thinking-mother creates a space for thinking in the infant's mind. In this way the baby first learns to think from being thought about, which lays the foundation for the development of the capacity to think.

If, however, because of her own anxieties, a mother is unable to fulfil this function for her baby, she may project her anxieties onto the baby rather than receiving and processing the baby's anxieties. This leads to confusion in the baby about which feelings are its own and which the mother's. This causes confusion in the baby's mind between self and mother. Bion suggests that the lack of a satisfactory early experience of having sensory impressions and emotions processed leads to difficulties in thinking. This, of course, causes difficulties in learning.

Modern research on the early development of the brain

Perry et al. describe findings, from modern neurological research on the early development of the brain, that neural pathways in the brain become sensitized by use. The more a response has been activated the more readily it can be activated again, so with repetition it can be activated by "decreasingly intense stimuli". In the case of traumatized children, their traumatic experiences lead to extreme sensitization of the response patterns connected with their traumatic experiences. Following this the hyper-aroused state may be triggered by stimuli that seem insignificant to others. This sort of child may, for example, react to another child accidentally bumping into him/her in the playground as if it were a dangerously threatening attack and over-react accordingly. Such children can be hyperactive, extremely anxious, and/or impulsive, and have physical symptoms or sleeping problems. Teachers sometimes perceive a child in this state as attacking other children for no reason, and tell them off for doing so, while the child perceives himself as under attack and acting in self-defence.

On the other hand, children who have reacted in the opposite way to trauma, by the "freeze" response, will often tend to freeze when they feel anxious. Small insignificant-seeming triggers can set off their anxiety. They may even be unaware at times of what has made them anxious, it can be something that is reminiscent, in an unconscious way, of their traumatic experience. In this state of frozen anxiety, they sometimes act as if they had not heard what they were asked to do. This is sometimes misunderstood as obstinacy or refusal to co-operate. If this happens, and they are told off about it, they will feel increasingly anxious and threatened and the freezing may develop into dissociation. They may become withdrawn and retreat into day-dreams and fantasies, cut off from what is going on around them.

Perry et al. highlighted the survival value of a state of hyper-arousal for children in a dangerous environment. They point out that the human brain and its functions develop in response to experience and that the brain has evolved "to perceive, process and act on information from the environment in order to maximise survival potential". They comment that having a hyper-vigilant arousal system has survival value for a child brought up in a dangerous environment, where the adults' behaviour towards the child is neglectful, unpredictable, unreliable, and/or violent. If a child is subjected to frequent physical abuse it is adaptive to react quickly to escape from the danger of attack, or to hit out before being hit. They suggest that the very characteristics of the developing brain that enable a child to learn quickly about the environment, in order to give the best chance of survival, eventually give away the child who has suffered traumatic experiences (Damasio, 1999; Emanuel, 2000; Perry et al., 1995).

Transference and countertransference

The concepts of transference and countertransference also play an important part in the work of educational psychotherapists. The basic theoretical concept involved here is that feelings, expectations, and attitudes, which children have developed within relationships at home tend to be imported into other relationships. Freud first discovered this phenomenon within the psychoanalytic relationship and named it "transference", but it also applies to relationships with teachers or educational psychotherapists and attitudes to learning shown within those relationships. Adults also have feelings about individual children with whom they work, in psychoanalytic terminology countertransference feelings. These include feelings the adult transfers from his/her previous relationships, but also those that a child's behaviour, attitude, or expressions of feeling stir up in the adult. Reflecting on one's "countertransference" feelings towards a child can sometimes help to recognize when feelings are being evoked, or provoked, in one by the child and to avoid falling into the trap of reacting automatically, in a way that reinforces dysfunctional patterns (Heimann, 1950).

An illustration of the application of psychoanalytic concepts of transference and countertransference can be seen in Peter's Educational Psychotherapy (see Chapter One).

In the teaching aspect of my relationship with Peter, I noticed, after a time, that whenever I pointed out directly that he had made a mistake, he would go on making that mistake for the rest of the session. I found, however, that if instead of saying, "No" or "You've got that word wrong", I said, "Try that word again"; or if he read the word "rain" as "ran" and I pointed to the word saying "Look, the letters 'ai' together in that word sound 'A' ", he was very receptive. In this case he was usually able to correct his mistake, remember, and retain what I had taught him and apply the newly acquired knowledge to other words, both in that session and subsequently. On the other hand I felt a lot of pressure on me from Peter to direct and control him. He expected me to do so and elicited that expectation, and the impulse to respond to it, in me. It felt exasperating when I had corrected a mistake and he went on repeating the mistake, as if he was just being contrary in stubbornly refusing to accept my teaching. I think he *was* in a way, but probably on a quite unconscious level. The major part of my work with him went into the effort involved in restraining myself and preventing myself becoming the controlling pushing person he expected and enticed me to be. I think this is a clear example of transference and countertransference.

I had strong evidence, from the occasional meetings I had with Peter's mother, that she was a very controlling, pressurizing mother. She was very angry with me on one occasion when Peter told her he had not done any reading at all in one session with me. We met to discuss this and she expressed her dissatisfaction on hearing that Peter had done no reading in that session, complaining that Peter did not concentrate enough and I should be *making* him read. It seemed clear that the feelings Peter had in relation to his mother were transferred to me, as doubtless they were to his teachers too, and he viewed me as wanting to control and push him. My countertransference reaction to this was to feel like controlling and pushing him. My observation and understanding of what was happening helped me to avoid this trap. Also, his reading made a sudden leap forward following that meeting with his mother, at which he was present. He heard me talk to her about how he found it very difficult to concentrate on reading for long, as he became very anxious. I had told her that at that stage I was very pleased if he concentrated for five minutes, as even that was a struggle for him. In Educational Psychotherapy with Peter I was aware of the transference phenomena and reacted to them by very deliberately behaving in a way unlike the way his transferred feelings led him to expect of me. By demonstrating very clearly, in my behaviour, that I was not the same as the controlling "mother–teacher" he had in mind and expected me to be, and relating to him differently, I was able to give him another kind of experience. This was, seemingly, quite a new experience for him and through it he developed autonomy. He was then able to learn in a way that was under his control to a large extent. Within this context he could be receptive to my giving him information and helping him with skills that he needed at the time. If he wanted to read a word, he was ready to learn the letter sounds he needed for that word. If, however, I tried to teach him letter sounds out of context he was incredibly resistant and we did not get very far. I did almost all the teaching of phonic skills with Peter in this incidental way. I also chose a reading series for him which was carefully graded phonically, which meant that new rules came up in the reading material gradually and in a progressive sequence and could be covered one by one in this incidental way. I could be sure, by controlling the reading material to this degree, that we would cover all the reading rules that Peter needed to know.

The relevance to teachers of the understanding of transference and countertransference

In taking seminars for teachers, in which they talk about their work with difficult children, I have learnt from their feedback that they find the concepts of transference and countertransference among the most helpful in making sense of what is going on in a difficult pupil–teacher relationship. If the teacher realizes, when a child is being particularly provocative in class, that the child's attitude originates in a difficult relationship with a parent, it can help the teacher to take it less personally. This makes it easier to contain the countertransference impulse to react to the child's provocation in a punitive manner that would confirm his expectation of a hostile response. Avoiding getting drawn into an automatic reaction to the child's provocation can enable the teacher to pause and reflect on what might be going on. Sometimes it is then possible to think of other ways to address the problem.

The effects of family interaction on children's learning

Later, Caspari became interested in family dynamics and the ways in which family concerns and interactions affect children's learning. One of these involved family secrets. John Bowlby contributed to the understanding of this area of learning inhibition from his discovery, through his psychoanalytic work with adult patients, of the effect on them of family secrets they were not supposed to know about as children (Bowlby, 1988a).

In a paper on "Educational Psychotherapy with a Latency Child" (Dover, 1996) Jenny Dover writes

> Many children seen in Educational Psychotherapy appear to develop satisfactorily and then stop learning at some point. This is often related to some recent trauma or environmental lapse. An example of this is John, who stopped reading when he inadvertently discovered that his brother was terminally ill. This information was supposed to be secret and unknown to him. Since John equated reading with accessing information, an intolerable internal conflict resulted. John already knew that his brother was ill, but overheard it mentioned that his brother would die of the illness and was not supposed to know this. When the secret was brought into the open in a family session at the clinic and John was, therefore, allowed to know about it, his reading progress resumed.

Muriel Barrett, who worked with Irene Caspari, as a Remedial Teacher and Educational Therapist at the Tavistock Clinic, has written about the application of Attachment Theory, in her work with children with emotionally based learning difficulties (Barrett & Trevitt, 1991). She continued to develop Educational Psychotherapy work at the Tavistock Clinic following Irene Caspari's death and described several secrets that had emerged during the course of Educational Psychotherapy with families, as follows:

> A father who was serving a prison sentence for his violent behaviour;
> a referred young person at 15, in trouble with the law, who came alone and told me he was "being done for GBH"; but had somehow kept this from his parents;
> a parent whose addiction to drugs did not remain secret when the children frequently missed their schooling.

Barrett comments, "there may be a fear that the fact the father has no work will come to light, that parents are violent towards each other or their children, or, even more seriously, that sexual abuse is being perpetrated."

Further examples of Educational Psychotherapy with families are given by Muriel Barrett in Chapter Eight: "Family Dynamics and the Educational Experience", where she describes joint work in which she and her colleagues involved parents in the work with their child who had learning difficulties. She conveys how parents in these families were often reluctant to think in terms of their involvement and simply wanted their child to have help with the learning difficulty.

The chapter illustrates how, by starting with a focus on the learning problem, it was possible to help some parents to see how their family relationships played a part in their child's inhibitions about learning and to help them modify their interactions with the child in a way that facilitated learning. Other parents were resistant to attempts to help them consider the part their family relationships played in their child's difficulties in learning. In some cases the work enabled them to modify their attitude, but in others the parents found it hard to consider their involvement in their child's problem and only managed to do so to a limited degree, if at all.

In Chapter Nine, "Therapeutic Story Groups: Educational Psychotherapy in a School Setting", Gill Morton writes about therapeutic group work with children in a mainstream school. She describes the model of group work she has developed, drawing on educational psychotherapy principles, in which she undertakes a time-limited series of sessions with a small group of children who are presenting difficulties in school. She also involves a member of the school's teaching staff in working alongside her in this work. By so doing she simultaneously offers a therapeutic opportunity for the children and a training opportunity for the teacher, who can learn how to adopt something of this approach in his/her work with children. The chapter describes how, in conjunction with the teacher, Morton runs therapeutic story groups, in which the children are invited to collaborate in making up a story together, which results in their producing a book at the end of the project.

Consultation to teachers

From the beginning, the development of Educational Psychotherapy and consultation to teachers have gone hand-in-hand. Irene Caspari was always keen to pass on to teachers, and to teacher trainers, insights she had gained through her psychological training and clinical experience of work with children, informed by psychoanalytic understanding. In the 1960s, for example, she was involved in supervising Diploma Course students at Leicester University who were supervising the teaching practice of final year student–teachers. Her emphasis was on getting the students to observe, reflect on, and describe what went on in their own lessons, including the interaction between their pupils and themselves. Gerda Hanko was influenced by Irene Caspari's work in Leicester and applied this approach to her work as an Educational Consultant by emphasizing collaborative thinking, to enable teachers to find solutions to problems, rather than adopting a directive, advice-giving stance (Hanko, 1999/2001).

In Chapter Ten, "What Can Educational Psychotherapy Teach Teachers?" Marie Delaney describes consultation work with the teaching staff in mainstream schools, in which the aim is to facilitate the teachers' thinking and understanding of the problems of children they work with, including their own feelings and reactions to the children. She sets out to bridge the gap between "teaching" and "therapy" that often seems to exist in the teachers' minds, outlining some of her strategies for introducing teachers to theoretical concepts and new ways of thinking about children's learning and behaviour problems, derived from her training and experience in Educational Psychotherapy. Her approach is aimed at helping the teachers develop and apply these new ways of thinking within their role as teachers.

She has also written books for teachers in mainstream schools: "Teaching the Unteachable" (Delaney, 2009) and "What can I do with the kid who...?" (Delaney, 2010).

CHAPTER THREE

The potential space and indirect communication in educational psychotherapy

Helen High

In his book *Playing and Reality* Winnicott put forward the idea that "psychotherapy takes place in the overlap of two areas of playing, that of the patient and that of the therapist. Psychotherapy has to do with two people playing together" (Winnicott, 1971a). He linked play with his concept of the transitional object, or a baby's "first not-me possession". The "transitional object" was the name Winnicott gave to

> The object to which a baby, at a certain stage of development, becomes especially attached, usually a soft object such as a cuddly toy or a bit of blanket or cloth. At this stage the infant often turns to this object, rather than part of its own body such as the thumb, as a means of self-soothing or comfort, at the time of going to sleep or when distressed.

He also described the transitional object as, "a symbol of the union of the baby and mother at the time they are becoming separate in the baby's mind". He suggested that, at times, play involves a special kind of reality that is different from both external and internal reality. In considering this Winnicott posed the question. "If play is neither inside nor outside, where is it?" His answer to his own question was that, as the baby and mother start to become separate in the baby's mind, a potential space arises between them in which play, language, a world of shared imagination, and communication through symbols can develop. He put forward the theory that cultural experience is a derivative of play, and, like play, takes place in a potential space between people. A work of art considered from this point of view is, like children's play, neither internal nor external reality, communicates through symbols and has a special kind of reality that is different from both external and internal reality.

Winnicott emphasized that "an essential feature of transitional phenomena and objects is a quality in our attitude when we observe them". In considering the favourite toy or bit of cloth to which a young child has become specially attached, he comments: "We agree never to make the challenge to the child *did you create this object or did you find it conveniently lying around?*".

The same goes for the creative arts. If, at the theatre, we are gripped by the performance and drawn into the drama enacted on the stage, we allow a time for this special kind of reality to go unchallenged. We suspend disbelief and enter into the experience of the events portrayed on the stage and the emotions and conflicts of the characters in the drama. These events and experiences take place in a potential space between the actors and the audience.

Likewise, educational psychotherapy takes place in a potential space between the educational psychotherapist and the child or adolescent (High, 1998). The use of play, drawing, stories, and suchlike, in educational psychotherapy, lends itself to communication in a way that is different from talking directly with children or adolescents about the external reality of their lives or their internal fantasies and feelings. When a child or adolescent is not ready to discuss feelings about difficult real life experiences directly, he/she may be able to express feelings indirectly, without the reality of what is expressed in this way being challenged. A very clear example of this was given by Elsie Osborne, who was Irene Caspari's successor as the Organizing Tutor of the Educational Psychology training at the Tavistock Clinic (Osborne, 1989). Elsie was working with a young boy whose family was breaking up. He literally did not know where he was going to be living next, or with whom. If he was asked how things were at home he could never bear to discuss the subject. He brushed it aside saying things were fine. In his educational psychotherapy sessions, however, he made up a serial story, illustrated by drawings, about a poor little donkey and the terrible things that kept happening to this little donkey. Osborne was then able to talk with him about how hard it was for this poor little donkey and to empathize with his suffering through the metaphor of the story. The child responded to this and entered into discussion about how the poor little donkey felt. This type of indirect approach allows the child to connect the therapist's understanding of the character in the story to their own situation if they are ready to, but to distance it from themselves and consider it out there in the metaphor if they are not.

Case illustration

Margaret, a tall 12-year-old, had been taken into Care following a terrifying incident in which her mentally ill mother had threatened her with a knife. She was living in a foster home as one of a group of children, where she was described as unco-operative in her attitude to the staff and aggressive to other children. In her sessions with me she could not bear to talk directly of her feelings about her situation, but one day she made a small plasticine model of a picture in a frame. She then made up a story about the picture being stolen by a boy from his brother. The picture was the brother's birthday present. I asked her to repeat the story so that I could write it down. The following is her story as she dictated it:

The Bad-tempered Brothers

Once upon a time there were two brothers, one was called Fred and the other was called Jim and one-day Fred got a parcel. It was from his friend because it was his birthday. It was a picture of a vase and some flowers in it and his brother was jealous so his brother stole the picture. Fred was angry, so he punched his brother in the eye and he had a black eye. Jim ran away into the woods. He stayed in the woods for a long time; it was scary in the woods because he thought there was a werewolf in there. Then he thought he would go back and apologise to his brother. So he did and they were friends again.

In the original version (made up as she went along before I suggested writing it down), when Jim ran away into the woods he was *angry* with Fred for punching him. There was no mention of it being scary in the woods and no mention of a werewolf. When we talked about the emotions of these brothers in the story Margaret was able to think about their feelings and enter into a discussion about them. In the discussion I suggested that Jim stole the picture because he was jealous it was Fred's birthday present and that made Fred angry and started the fight. I said I thought it was Jim's jealous feelings that had caused all the trouble. She was receptive to this idea and able to reflect on it and discuss the emotions involved. She could think about jealousy giving rise to difficult behaviour when we communicated indirectly, through the metaphor of her story, although she could not at that stage take open discussion of the jealous rivalry that gave rise to her aggressive behaviour in the children's home. The story was, of course, *her* story, she had made it up and expressed the feelings in it, but she had expressed them in this indirect way, which freed her to discuss the feelings and think about them unselfconsciously. Also, in regarding this story in the special way in which Winnicott thought of the child's transitional object, I did not challenge Margaret by asking "is this real?" or "does this really apply to you and your behaviour?"

The value of indirect exploration of feelings in expression work

This indirect exploration of feelings in expression work can enable some children, who have previously been unable to do so, to begin to think about feelings and behaviour and the links between them. On the one hand, this can help children who have been inhibited and unable to express or even think about certain feelings. Where these inhibitions have interfered with the child's learning, finding a safe vehicle to express, say, dangerous hostile and aggressive impulses, can free up the child's ability to learn. Equally, on the other hand, this kind of symbolic expression of dangerous or unacceptable feelings can help children who tend to act out unthinkingly, to find a way to process their feelings. They can learn to symbolize their difficult and troubling emotions rather than evacuating them through action. This applied to Margaret who had been inclined to tyrannize other children and justify her behaviour, rather than acknowledge her distress, anger, fear, her jealousy of other children and suchlike complicated and difficult-to-bear emotions. I could only work with Margaret for a limited period of time, approximately six months, but already they were finding her somewhat more contained and less aggressive in her behaviour in the foster home. A fuller account of Margaret's educational therapy is given in an earlier article (High, 1985).

The relevance of story themes to specific problems

In this indirect way, particular kinds of story may help children facing particular situations, as in the following examples: A story with a hero who protects others from attack may carry a reassuring message for a child struggling with powerful ambivalent feelings, anxious that his/ her aggressive feelings and impulses may overpower and destroy the loving and caring ones. A story whose theme is divided loyalty may have a particular emotional significance for a child who is attached to both parents when they are in process of divorcing, or already divorced. It may sometimes be easier for a child who is going through a very painful time over the parents' divorce, to think and talk about a loyalty conflict in a story, which is not about divorce as such. To talk about the subject directly may be too close to home.

The choice of a theme to fit a child's particular emotional conflict is also an indirect communication from the educational psychotherapist, that the conflict can be thought about. It gives the child permission to explore feelings indirectly, through the metaphor of the story. It does also offer the opportunity for the child to make conscious links with their personal situation if and when they feel ready to do so.

Communication through errors and the use of games in educational psychotherapy

Sometimes children communicate indirectly through the type of mistake they make. Irene Caspari (1974a) quoted an example of a boy whose educational psychotherapist she was supervising. At a particular point the child started to make mistakes by frequently reading words backwards. He read *"on"* as *"no"* for instance and *"was"* as *"saw"*. He had never made this kind of error before, so he was not incapable of distinguishing the direction of words. This type of mistake persisted over several sessions, then one day he tried to read the word *"empty"* backwards. By tackling this word in reverse he was trying to make sense of *"ytpme"*, which presented him with a great deal of difficulty. At this point the educational psychotherapist stopped reading and suggested they play a game. She had concluded that in reading words backwards the child was expressing opposition to her, as she knew he was capable of reading the words correctly. She introduced a drawing game of opposites in which she drew a picture of rain and asked the boy to draw the opposite. He then drew a picture for her to draw the opposite. The game developed until the drawings depicted feelings like happiness and sadness, building up and destruction by fire. In the next session the boy's tendency to reverse had disappeared and was never a problem again. By introducing the game of opposites the educational psychotherapist communicated, indirectly, to the boy that she understood he needed to express his opposition to her. The game gave him permission to do so and provided a vehicle that allowed him to express opposing emotions in a playful way. After this indirect way of exploring and expressing his opposition and ambivalence he no longer needed to do so through the previous indirect means of reversing words while reading.

Games may be used in a number of ways to address emotional issues in educational psychotherapy. Structured games with rules can play a useful part. These, of course, usually appeal to children over a certain age.

Competitive Games provide a channel for expressing rivalry and aggression in a socially acceptable way. Anxieties and inhibitions about rivalry and aggression are prominent among children whose emotional problems inhibit their learning. Some are afraid to compete for fear of losing and some are afraid to triumph by winning, as they feel guilty about humiliating their opponents and experience winning as a destructive act. It is difficult for children who have such intense conflicts about winning and losing to work things out in competitive games with their peers, who may sometimes be very triumphant about winning or upset about losing. They may think of learning as a competition with their peers and be so preoccupied with the other children's performance in class, as compared with their own, that it distracts them from their studies and hinders their progress.

Competitive games used in educational psychotherapy

In educational psychotherapy competitive games may be played between the child and the educational psychotherapist, who does not, on the whole, mind losing. In certain games it is possible to arrange things so that the child has a good chance of winning. This is important for children who are unbearably demoralized by repeated failure and feel they are always losers. Caspari (1986) devised an ingenious scoring system to use with individual children in conjunction with a learning task. In this scoring system, each time the child succeeds in an item of the learning task, such as reading a word, he or she scores a point, or is allowed a turn to move in a board game. The educational psychotherapist scores a point or makes a move only when the child fails an item. In this way the child is given permission to express aggressive, competitive feelings by beating the therapist in the game, but can only do so by succeeding in learning. The child's chance of success can be controlled in this type of game by setting tasks that, at first, are relatively easy and introducing new learning gradually, at a pace adapted to the child's needs, as I did with Peter (see Chapter One). There is then enough challenge to stretch the child a little at a time. Failure only comes in small doses and there is enough experience of success to build confidence by making it possible for the child to win most games. The difficulty of the tasks can be adjusted to the child's rate of progress. In beating the educational psychotherapist in the game a child knows that the therapist is pleased about their success in the learning task. This puts them in the position of simultaneously opposing and co-operating with the therapist or, as Caspari described it, puts them in "a benign double-bind". This set-up provides an ideal vehicle for the expression of ambivalent feelings. By linking the score to a game with an aggressive content, the therapist communicates even more clearly that ambivalent feelings are tolerable. The child can experience it as acceptable, safe, and even fun to express aggressive feelings indirectly through the game; to have a playful fight, as it were, expressing hostility and enjoying an activity together simultaneously. The child who needs help with reading, spelling or mathematics cannot, of course, compete directly on equal terms with an adult in a reading, spelling or number game. By using the scoring system described earlier, however, the child is sure to win if he succeeds in the learning task. This device can be equally successful with a child who is afraid of losing and a child who is afraid of winning. The child who feels he is a hopeless loser in his failure to learn is encouraged by the experience of success. A child who is worried about humiliating or destroying an opponent knows that the educational psychotherapist is pleased when he/she succeeds in the game, because it means the child is learning. Although the therapist is losing the game s/he is succeeding in the teaching, so both are winners in a way.

Caspari also commonly used the game "hang-the-man", in conjunction with this scoring system, as a socially acceptable way for children who are anxious about their aggressive fantasies to express aggression in a symbolic, safe, and enjoyable manner. In the game "hang-the-man", whenever a player scores a point s/he draws one part of a gallows, or of the human body hanging on the gallows. The player who first completes his drawing of a hanged man wins the game and is said to have hanged his or her opponent. By introducing this game the educational psychotherapist indirectly gives the child permission to "kill" her symbolically, conveying that the indirect expression of violent feelings in the game is acceptable and can even be fun. Linked to the learning task in this way, the aggression is expressed in the service of learning rather than inhibiting it (Caspari, 1974a, pp. 215–232; Caspari, 1986, pp. 50–65). I find this type of game and scoring system particularly successful with children who are resistant to one's efforts to teach them. They can make you feel as if they are stubbornly refusing to learn, as Peter made me feel. Sometimes these children are locked into a competitive battle where they defeat your efforts by failing to learn. They unconsciously attack and undermine the teacher's effectiveness by their resistance and can make you feel demoralized and defeated. However, in the type of competitive game just described, linked to an educational task, the only way the child can defeat you is by succeeding in the learning task.

"Once upon a time": the symbolic meaning of fairy tales and their use in educational psychotherapy

Gillian Salmon

As Christmas approached, it seemed timely to read the story of "The Little Christmas Tree" with my Educational Psychotherapy group. It was from a "reader" of the time and told of three trees of differing sizes growing on a hill. Each is approached by a bird, lost and in need of a branch to rest. The largest tree and the middle-sized tree both refuse him a place on the grounds that they expect to be Christmas trees. The smallest tree welcomes the bird, who then creeps close to the trunk of the tree and begins to feel better. Just at this point, along comes Santa Claus in his sleigh and, bypassing the large and middle-sized trees, he stops in front of the smallest tree. He remarks on how pretty it is and chooses it for a Christmas tree, taking with it the resident bird.

Three of the four children in the group made comments about the moral of the story—the implication that virtue is rewarded. The fourth, Gina, sat looking very thoughtful and quite concerned. She voiced her worry, which was about what would happen to the smallest tree when it was uprooted from the forest. She feared it would die. The simple answer was that if the tree were moved with some of the surrounding soil, its roots would be protected and it could flourish. Underlying Gina's anxiety, however, was the fact that she had come with her Cypriot family, to live in UK, less than three years before. The story seemed to be a metaphor for the sense of displacement that she experienced and her fear that the experience could do her lasting harm. There are many stories that similarly offer a metaphor for some part of the child's experience and can allow re-thinking of concerns because they are not being discussed so directly as to be overwhelmingly distressing.

Bruno Bettelheim was a child psychologist who had grown up in Vienna and underwent psychoanalysis there. He spent over a year in concentration camps and, after his release, went to the United States of America where he became involved in a project at the University of Chicago. In 1944, he accepted the post of Director of the Orthogenic School attached to the University. Here, he developed an approach to working with young people who were considered emotionally disturbed and in need of help to develop capacities that would allow them to control their aggressive impulses, to manage their anxiety, and to address other areas of difficulty in their functioning. The approach was called "milieu therapy" and was psychoanalytically oriented. The environment was designed to offer warmth, consistency, and relief from the stress of ordinary life and this was reflected in the building itself, where great efforts were made to create a meaningful built environment.

One of the ways in which he promoted the development of the children attending the school was by encouraging their ability to read, because he recognized that this ability had "a unique importance in the process of education". He railed, in "On Learning to Read", against the emptiness of many of the early readers produced for children and advocated reading material that respected the "intelligence and dignity" of the child and that presented reading as intrinsically interesting (Bettelheim & Zelan, 1981). He recognized that, for a story to hold a child's attention it must entertain and excite curiosity, but to be truly enriching, it must also stimulate the imagination and suggest solutions to problems experienced in regard to all aspects of the personality. Many adults feel that children should be diverted from troubling thoughts and violent fantasies, but if the dark side of their natures is not recognized as being within, the process of projecting it into things or people outside of the self becomes the only way of dealing with these anxieties.

He identified a number of ideas and dilemmas that need to be addressed as the child grows up. Among these are the following:

- The unconscious powerfully influences behaviour and if its content is not recognized, and is therefore repressed, the personality can be distorted and the conscious mind overwhelmed.
- At some stages, these unconscious thoughts need to be externalized in order to make them bearable. If they are then projected into other things or people, rather than into symbolic characters in a story, the world can become a very frightening place.
- It is necessary to learn more about the world than can be directly experienced, but sorting the impressions gained into a coherent picture of the world requires the ability to distinguish between reality and fantasy.
- The individual struggles to achieve psychological maturity by facing many developmental crises and must recognize that this may involve encountering severe difficulties, but that they can be overcome.
- Among these crises is the rivalry experienced towards siblings.
- Another and most important crisis is the need, ultimately, to become a person who is independent of the parents and free from the power he, as a young child, invested in them.
- The child has to answer the question of what sort of a person s/he is to become.
- The fact that both evil and good are always present has to be recognized. Making choices involves being aware of what is meaningful and appropriate for the self. This can then lead to the inner integration of our ambivalence.
- The making of good choices is more likely to be based on identification with an interesting hero than on an abstract code.

Bettelheim (1976) understood that folk fairy tales, that had often been part of an oral tradition for generations, had absorbed the conscious and unconscious feelings of both tellers and listeners and presented them in symbolic form. They offered accounts of events, which might be fantastical, but were told in a manner that suggested they were relating the everyday and could be part of the experience of anyone. In this way they differed from myths, which told of remarkable and spectacular events and which also usually ended in tragedy. Fairy tales, on the other hand, were resolved in a "happy ending". Most of the characters in fairy tales are un-named and known only by their relationship with the central character. The central character in turn is usually given a symbolic name such as "Cinderella" representing her position as one who stays by the hearth and "Jack" representing any boy. These characters encounter a range of situations with which the reader can identify, but which present symbolic images for the solution of their difficulties.

Fairy tales are often retold in very simplified form but Bettelheim recommended that they should be told in their traditional complexity so that they allowed the hearer to gain from their richness and imaginative content. His experience of reading them with children convinced him that they were a very powerful tool in enabling the child to deal with some of the tensions and major developmental processes with which s/he struggled. He recognized that not all fairy stories cover every aspect of the child's needs and identified some that were especially relevant at particular stages of the child's development. He also made this point in relation to adult reading in "Recollections and Reflections" (Bettelheim, 1992).

Among the fairy stories that deal with particular issues and are widely available the following are briefly described:

- "The Three Little Pigs" tells of the way in which the urge to seek only pleasure can be modified by being in touch with reality and developing the skills and qualities that allow mastery over it. Each of the little pigs is a representation of part of the individual and the wolf is also an externalization of the greedy devouring instinct that the child is ultimately able to overcome.

- "Cinderella" in its present form speaks most clearly of sibling rivalry and the experience of having a difficult time, with which many children can identify. There is a helpful "fairy godmother", who symbolizes the basic trust that has been instilled in the child by early good "mothering" and allows the idealized "good mother" to be internalized despite contact with the "bad stepmother", who is so punitive and demanding. Following the hardships imposed on her by having to submit to the harshness of her siblings and her stepmother, Cinderella is able to survive her anxieties about her own possible inadequacy. She achieves autonomy and a happy sexual union symbolized by the fitting of the slipper on her foot by the prince.

- "Goldilocks and the Three Bears" does not have all the features of a traditional fairy tale. It tells of Goldilocks' efforts to learn what kind of a person she can be and to play various roles as she explores this. The story presents a well-integrated family, but does not suggest how she integrates the different aspects of her personality or makes the transition to adulthood.

- "Sleeping Beauty" tells of the importance of a period of quiet growth before the attainment of sexual maturity. It describes the father's attempt to protect her from sexual awakening by the dense hedge and the small room in which she is kept and gives an account of the stages through which the female must progress to achieve self-fulfilment.

- "Little Red Riding Hood", like the "Three Little Pigs" tells of the choice the child must make between following pleasure and taking account of reality. Again there is a wolf, representing the asocial and animalistic urges within the self and, again, they are conquered. This time it is the figure of the hunter who helps to deal with this. He uses reason rather than emotion and is thus more of a parental figure.

- "Jack and the Beanstalk" speaks of the boy having to attain maturity by using his potency, by setting constructive goals, and by developing artistic accomplishments. The parental figures do not see that he is dealing with the problems of his developing maturity and he has to vanquish the ogre who can be seen as the oedipal father.

- "Snow White", like many fairy tales, deals with the oedipal problem and suggests that the parent who has failed to integrate as a child, symbolized by the jealous stepmother, has more difficulty in recognizing the need of their own child to grow up. It is difficult for the child to achieve more than the parent because s/he may fear retribution. In Snow White's case, she withdraws from the contest by trying to escape to a more infantile stage but, eventually, after a period of "sleep", her sexuality is awakened when she is intellectually and emotionally ready for such an adult relationship.

Case illustrations

The story of "Hansel and Gretel" addresses the separation anxiety that is associated with the fear of being abandoned by the parents and the fear of starvation that encourages greed. It offers an opportunity to think about the resourcefulness of the children in the face of their rejection by the parents and the way in which satisfying and mature relationships within the family are developed in the longer term.

(a) Sarah, who was eight years old, had great difficulty in separating from her mother and in being able to learn successfully. She had experienced the break-up of her parents' marriage and the abduction of her older sister from the family home by her father. Her mother had then gone overseas to try to bring her elder daughter back and so Sarah had temporarily lost her too.

After some weeks of working together in Educational Psychotherapy and when she felt that a trusting relationship had been established, her therapist introduced the story of "Hansel and Gretel". She listened to several different versions of the story without responding initially, but gradually she began to comment on the story, commenting that, perhaps the stepmother and the witch were the same person as both had died. She used small figures to enact some of the scenes from the story and was eventually able to invest them with some of her more aggressive and cruel feelings. She continued to play with these and other figures for several weeks and her therapist then made a track game that used the story for some of the locations on the track. This became a game in which Sarah could be very excited and act out some of her most angry feelings, although within the structure of the game and within the content of the story. In this way she was able to safely act out some of her ambivalence and hatred towards the adults who had caused her such distress and this allowed her to begin to be able to take advantage of her learning opportunities in school.

(b) A twelve-year-old girl, Eve, was seen for Educational Psychotherapy because she had attempted suicide and was also failing to attend school regularly or to succeed in any of the learning opportunities it offered (Gomnaes, 1988). Eve's parents had been divorced for six years and there had been many disputes about where she, the youngest of three, would live. There had, therefore, been many changes of home and school for her, and her two older siblings were living elsewhere. Her therapist felt that she was highly intelligent, but hypersensitive and found it difficult to trust adults, as she perceived any positive feedback as being untrue, but put up a barrier between herself and any teacher who pointed out errors and offered help. Eve herself described having "black holes", but it was clear that she was unable to take in anything that could help to fill them. It became clear that Eve had artistic talent and in an early session her therapist asked her to draw a picture of a miraculous house, having previously told her that she would tell her a fairy tale that she could illustrate. Her therapist thought at first that the picture she drew was of Sleeping Beauty's castle, but Eve explained that it was the castle associated with Rapunzel. In the following session the story was read and Eve began to illustrate it.

The story tells of a husband and wife who lived next door to a wicked enchantress, who longed for a child. When the wife found that she was to have a child she craved the rapunzel in this woman's garden. Her husband, desperate to please her, stole some and when he went back for more, found himself face to face with the enchantress who obliged him to promise, in return for a constant supply of the vegetable, to give her whatever she asked once the baby was born. When the time came, the enchantress claimed the baby and brought her up, locked in a tall tower from the age of twelve, to keep her away from the world. She called her Rapunzel and the girl grew wonderful long gold hair. The enchantress climbed up this to visit her. When a handsome prince passed by, he was enraptured by Rapunzel's singing and eventually discovered the way in. The enchantress found out that he was visiting Rapunzel and banished her to the desert where she bore the prince a son and daughter and lived in great hardship until he found her after long searching. They lived happily for many years.

"Rapunzel" illustrates the nature and consequences of desire and ways in which the child can make use of its own resources to deal with the difficult situations it faces. It is a much more intricate story than the one illustrated at the beginning of this chapter, and so it allows exploration of a range of complex feelings and of alternative courses of action. Bettelheim notes that the story symbolizes the transfer of a relationship established with the parents, to that of a lover (Bettelheim, 1976). There are accounts of selfish behaviour, of betrayal of love, of periods of trial and tribulation, and of sheer fantasy. Eve was able to use the story to stimulate a series of paintings to which she added her own commentary. She painted pictures of things that were genuine and things that were false. She illustrated the greedy feeling in the wife who wanted the rapunzel plant, but was also able to speak of her loneliness and her feeling of helplessness. She explored the way in which the husband and wife seemed compelled to meet their own needs and were obliged to give up their daughter because they could not put her needs first. She was also able, towards the end of the sessions, to think about the issues of separation and loss, which were pertinent to her own experience of the recent loss of her grandfather as well as to the therapy. Her therapist was aware that she was relating much of what she found in the story to her own life situation, but in their discussion, she and Eve remained within the framework of the story throughout. In this way, Eve could safely explore feelings that were unbearably painful, and, at the time, getting in the way of her learning. Although she and her family needed to have further help, she was then able to resume her education more successfully.

These two examples show how fairy tales stimulated the children concerned to consider and express feelings associated with their own experience. Neither was encouraged to relate the fairy tales to their own situation, but each was able to focus on, and identify with, the characters in the fairy tales. In this way they were not invited to learn a correct way to behave in relation to a particular circumstance, but were able to consider a situation from several points of view, to consider distressing feelings and ideas through their symbolic representations in the characters in the story, and to develop their own solutions to their problems.

PART II

EDUCATIONAL PSYCHOTHERAPY CASE STUDIES

CHAPTER FIVE

Work with a hard-to-reach child

Jenny Dover

Nine-year-old Matthew, recently received into Care, was playing a board game with me in his educational therapy session. The card he picked up demanded an answer to the question "When I need a hug I go to...". Matthew looked anxious. Then he brightened "I know", he said, "I won't need a hug!" This was his solution to a world where adults proved unreliable and unresponsive to his needs.

Although bright and potentially able, Matthew was seriously underachieving at school. His teacher described him as "preoccupied, distant, and rather lifeless". Matthew neither sought nor welcomed help with his work, preferring to struggle alone, and she was left feeling intrusive and rejected. In terms of Ainsworth's attachment typology (Ainsworth & Wittig, 1969) Matthew might be considered an avoidant anxiously attached child. He would have been an infant who turned away from the rejecting mother—defending against emotional pain through an imagined self- sufficiency.

I am going to describe an aspect of my individual work with Matthew in a Child and Family Consultation Service. I hope to demonstrate the way in which the relatively structured nature of educational psychotherapy, with its emphasis on indirect exploration of experience and on the task, was a particularly helpful intervention for this child.

Six months into the therapy Matthew was still unable to remember my name and frequently confused it with names of an array of social workers that had peopled his life in the last few years. By forgetting my name and confusing me with others, he gave me a flavour of what it felt like to be in a foster home with a large number of other children who came and went.

Matthew's "family" drawing depicted a sofa with a row of identical heads, seen from behind, watching a blank television set. Studies on the distinctive features of family drawings relating to patterns of attachment, suggest that it is typical of an avoidant child to draw his family showing little relation to each other or individuality. If a mother is included in the drawing, she may be hidden or disguised. Resistant or enmeshed children, in contrast, might draw figures close together or separated by a barrier of some sort. Secure children tend to differentiate family members and to show them interacting (Goldberg, 2000).

Matthew seemed surprised when I showed interest in his place in the family and I asked which head depicted which child. His sense of individuality was poorly developed. He found it hard to think about his own preferences or habits or to tell me about his current or past experience outside of the therapy room. The difficulty in expressing a coherent narrative of life typifies children who are insecurely attached.

When Matthew drew a picture of himself, his body was in profile, as if attempting to escape notice. His facial portrait was minimalist—although chilling in what it unwittingly revealed. Although Matthew showed no affect when producing the picture, I felt horror. There was no mouth and a strikingly phallic nose. Matthew had not spoken about his father's oral sexual abuse but his brother had done so.

Drawings can be a useful source of information in several ways. The graphic sexual quality of Matthew's self-portrait suggested that the experience of abuse remained unprocessed. It was more like a flashback or reproduction of the experience. Children who have processed the experience more successfully tend to find symbolic ways of indicating abuse. For example, they may draw attention to the genital area of their figure drawings, by drawing hearts and bows on the clothing (Moore, 1990).

Ears were also omitted in Matthew's picture and it was likely that his distress in the past had largely gone unheard. The absence of ears may also suggest the desire not to hear painful things. The blank TV screen too made me wonder about Matthew's desire to blank out memories and feelings. It seemed likely that the abuse compounded Matthew's early attachment difficulties.

Matthew was the second of three brothers who had lived with his learning disabled, schizophrenic mother and alcoholic father. The children, while living with their parents, suffered from serious neglect, and neighbours reported that the father would send his small sons out into the streets to forage for food. They were punished severely if they returned empty handed.

The boys' father was violent and unpredictable and the boys were afraid of him. In Care the eldest boy wet himself on an occasion when he glimpsed him in the street. Monitored visits with the father were terminated when he abused his youngest son in the toilet on one occasion. After this their father harassed the new Carers and the foster family moved to a new address to escape his threatening visits.

Cummings and Davies (1994) wrote "Domestic violence is a particularly potent source of developmental problems precisely because the fear of harm coming to the parent leads to anticipations of unavailability, confirmed by the inaccessibility of the mother at moments of acute marital conflict".

Research suggests too that the early experience of chronic violence and abuse may also have consequences for brain development, when parts of the brain responsible for activating survival mechanisms become overdeveloped and sensitized—at the expense of the more thoughtful reflective ones.

Nonetheless, during their assessment by the social services, all three boys expressed a desire to be returned to their father's care, demonstrating how powerful attachment to an abusive parent can be.

All three boys showed signs of emotional disturbance. Matthew was said to be undemanding and well-behaved, but he suffered nocturnal enuresis and was extremely reserved and uncommunicative. His social worker quickly abandoned the attempt to do "life story" work with him. He was also reluctant to engage with the staff in school, where, as described earlier, he tended to make himself "invisible" and reject help.

Interestingly, Matthew's foster mother, usually a warm and caring woman, found herself enraged by the enuresis, experiencing it as an aggressive act. She may have been re-enacting an inability in his birth mother to bear his negative feelings. Learning demands the comfortable use of aggression and Matthew's passivity, inside and outside of the therapy, was striking. It may be that he communicated his experience of rejection by eliciting these feelings in his foster mother. Wetting the bed when his guard was down at night seemed the closest he came to tears.

Matthew's foster mother said she found his silence intolerable—describing him as "looking at her funnily". I wondered about his birth mother's mental illness. What did Matthew see when he looked at her? Children learn about mental states by exploring the mind of the caregiver—but if what they see there is incomprehensible, terrifying or painful, they may repudiate this knowledge.

Bowlby suggested that different patterns of attachment affect the degree of access to certain kinds of thoughts, feelings, and memories. For example avoidant models of attachment permit only limited access to attachment-related thoughts. Avoidant children tend to trust cognition/logic more than resistant children, because, unlike them, they can predict parental response that has been consistently rejecting.

It seemed that Matthew's unconscious memory of past repeated interactions with his parent was being re-enacted in his relationships with adults—foster mother, teacher, and myself.

In the early sessions Matthew made no spontaneous communication and clearly found being alone in the room with me a strain. I was struck by his need to keep me at arm's length. He seemed to erect a "brick wall" between us and quickly made me feel terribly intrusive and a bit like a persecutor. He was more comfortable with a task or activity on which to focus. His preference was for factual science books although he appeared to listen very intently when I chose to read fairy stories or myths. He was compliant and inexpressive, showing no frustration when, for instance, the wooden house he was building came to pieces.

I tried not to be over-bright, in an attempt to enliven Matthew, and to consider carefully what he could tolerate. In view of the chronic abuse he had suffered it seemed important to provide an experience of non-intrusiveness and control in the therapy (Alvarez, 1992).

I, therefore, had two aims in my work with Matthew:

- to find a comfortable and tolerable way of "communicating with the past" and processing experiences
- the second—and perhaps more important—was the task of giving him a different experience of "self with other" (Stern, 1985/98).

The opportunity for this presented itself one day when, instead of offering a stimulus or a suggestion for writing a story, I wrote "Once upon a time..." and said, "Over to you." To my surprise Matthew was willing—even eager—to decide on the themes of his own stories and, provided I did not interfere in any way, to dictate them to me.

This activity was to be the vehicle for our work—the story providing a "buffer" between us that seemed important.

Story making is only one of the many projective techniques in an educational psychotherapist's armoury. It can be extraordinarily useful in a number of ways, apart from allowing fragile children to explore and express experience in the metaphor.

Stories can provide information about a child's inner world, characteristic conflicts, and preferred defensive adaptations. Secure children's stories differ from insecure children's insofar as they tend to contain realistic strategies, be peopled by well-meaning, responsible adults, and have appropriate feeling and resolution. The ways in which they change during therapy enable us to evaluate the children's progress.

Story making with Matthew related to my two aims. The *content* of the stories allowed an indirect means of reflecting safely on his past experience. The *process* of creating them alongside me gave him a new way of being with an adult.

Matthew chose the story-making activity every week and the sessions gained a sense of continuity, routine, and safety.

At first I played little part in creating the stories apart from sometimes noticing aloud and scribing as Matthew dictated them. It felt rather as if I was just an extra limb—an extension of him. I added nothing of my own, but each week, as we began, I recalled the previous week's events in the story linking past and present.

In my sessions with Matthew I hoped to recreate the conditions favourable for early learning within a relationship. Winnicott (1971a) proposed that a child needs to play alone in the presence of the mother if a stable true sense of self is to emerge. She must be sufficiently unobtrusive for the child to forget her and focus on self-exploration that lies at the root of solitary play.

Winnicott said that there were three conditions for the evolution of symbolic functioning in the transitional space between infant and caregiver:

- A sense of safety associated with experiencing the inner world
- An opportunity for the infant deliberately to limit concern with external events
- An opportunity to generate spontaneous creative gestures

This corresponds to Bowlby's concept of a secure base.

There is a lot of support for the view that therapeutic change is not so much a consequence of insight or reflection on episodic memory, but a consequence of repeated experiences that change procedural (implicit) memory. Stern (1995/98) suggests that these experiences are the building blocks of internal working models.

There were many stories in Matthew's repertoire, but the theme was always similar. The following story (which I paraphrase here) seemed key:

> There were three princes who lived with their parents, the king and queen, in their palace. The king was an angry man. He sent the princes out into the forest to search for treasure. He told them that if they returned without the treasure they would be killed. The forest was dark and horrible and full of terrible dangers. The princes had to struggle with dragons, snake pits, wild animals, witches in order to reach the treasure. Getting back to the palace was beset with difficulties.

Matthew had found a metaphor for his own experiences.

I was struck by the extraordinary contrast between the richness, imagery, and movement in these stories and the empty, bleak material he produced in response to being asked about himself directly.

Matthew's stories clearly contained elements of fairy tales (See Chapter Four). Bettelheim (1976) wrote about the very special meaning that these have for children.

He said,

> In order to master the psychological problems of growing up—overcoming narcissistic disappointments, oedipal dilemmas, sibling rivalries; becoming able to relinquish childhood dependencies; gaining a feeling of self worth, and a sense of moral obligation—a child needs to understand what is going on within his conscious self so that he can also cope with that which goes on in his unconscious. He can achieve this understanding, and with it the ability to cope, not through rational comprehension of the nature and content of his unconscious, but by becoming familiar with it through spinning out daydreams—ruminating, rearranging, and fantasizing about suitable story elements in response to unconscious pressures. By doing this, the child fits unconscious content into conscious fantasies, which then enable him to deal with that content.

Through the stories, Matthew and I were able to explore a number of issues in his experience—perhaps reliving the trauma in the only safe way available. Some of these issues were the huge struggle for survival—unsupported and against huge odds; the princes' desire to please the king whom they both loved and feared; the need to develop new survival skills, and to manage impossible situations; the power struggle but need for cooperation between the three brothers.

The relative lack of emotion in these stories was striking. The description of the princes' struggle was largely on a physical and not a psychological level. There was little reference to feelings in the characters.

This is reminiscent of adults who describe past abuse with total lack of affect. They are at greatest risk of revisiting their abusive past histories on their children. Fonagy et al. (1994) said "the caregiver's capacity to reflect the child's psychological experience provides him with part of the mental equipment necessary to establish his own reflective self...."

It seems that enabling children to experience our thinking about them—their intentions and their feelings—can also enable them to create internal working models of themselves, as thinking and feeling individuals.

A recurring theme in Matthew's stories was "finding a way back". Often he would illustrate this by drawing complex mazes leading back to the castle. This seemed linked to Matthew's expressed desire to return to his father, but also a sense of having lost something important early on and the painful difficulty of relocating it. Later I wondered if this also related to the weekly gap in the therapy sessions.

Another theme that came up repeatedly was about a queen trapped in a tower with a terrible monster and needing to be rescued by the princes. This may have reflected Matthew's anxiety about his learning disabled mother who was now alone with his father.

A story about a young hedgehog that was attacked by a larger one seemed to relate to Matthew's threatening father. Interestingly, the saviour, an owl who swoops down and removes the young hedgehog from harm, is seen as a punitive character (possibly his foster mother or me).

At first in the stories the princes rely on magical solutions. For example, the heroic second prince develops super powers, killing off everyone at a stroke. Children like Matthew, who have never experienced powerfulness or potency, may need to experience this imaginatively. Later, a wizard who granted him wishes, albeit unreliably, comes to his aid. I hoped this meant that Matthew was gaining a sense of outside support.

As time went on there was a gradual feeling of writing being a useful tool and a developing capacity in Matthew to allow me some of my own thoughts if they married with his overall ideas. He insisted we distinguish our ideas by using different coloured pens for this. I began to wonder aloud what the princes might *decide* to do—how they might *plan* a way to get out of a fix—in an attempt to emphasize a sense of agency in the princes. We began to debate suggestions about the action.

Incorporating my ideas into Matthew's imaginative world felt like the beginning of mutual play. We were co-constructing a shared experience and view of the world through the narrative. Some months into the work, Matthew agreed to share the scribing.

Over time there was an interesting shift in the stories. Now the princes had to rely on "cunning and trickery" rather than magic and to find their own strategies and solutions. The second prince puzzles, "What can I use which won't melt in the volcano?—I know...".

I felt Matthew had a corresponding growing sense of his own intelligence and ability.

We now entered a period where it felt comfortable enough to disagree about actions and how someone might behave—and it felt important to acknowledge openly with Matthew that we could have different ideas and ways of seeing things. I felt that this separation was possible because we had in some sense come together.

Interestingly, at the end of the story, the prince notices that the wizard's shoes are the same as the king's, and that they are one and the same person. Perhaps Matthew was developing a more integrated view of a father who was both good and bad.

The use of Matthew's story for reading purposes and using key words from his story for spelling gave Matthew a sense of control over his learning and increased his sense of himself. His preference for making up his own stories—rather than using existing ones—fitted better with his need for self-sufficiency and protection against intrusion. Even quite a long way into the work he preferred creating stories to hearing others.

Matthew remained a reserved individual who was guarded in his relationships. However, his sense of himself as a learner and thinker increased and the school began to report a greater interest and curiosity academically.

I hope this article has demonstrated the usefulness of using metaphor when working with an emotionally fragile child. It enabled him to communicate and think about painful past experience indirectly and to regulate the distance from the teacher/therapist through the structure of the task.

CHAPTER SIX

The effect of loss on learning: the stillborn sibling

Mia Beaumont

T his chapter examines the effect that the unmourned loss of a stillborn child has on other members of the family. It concentrates on the children who follow after the stillbirth and the difficulties they have with learning. It is based mainly on my own clinical experience, with reference to other writings on the subject. I have worked over the last six years with four children who have followed a stillbirth and with four who have lost a sibling.

In families where there has been a failure to mourn a stillbirth it is commonly found that subsequent children have difficulties with living and often with learning. Many ambivalent feelings surrounding the incompletely mourned loss remain in the family, particularly in the mother. These may be picked up by the child, and cause problems later.

Theoretical background to thinking about these issues

In Freud's classic description of melancholia (1917), he suggested that the patient had unconsciously lost an object for which he had had ambivalent feelings of love and hatred. The internalization of these negative feelings results in a lowering of self-esteem and ideas of self-denigration and self-punishment. Freud suggested that what distinguished melancholia from mourning was a lowering of "self-regard to a degree that finds utterance in self-reproaches and self-revilings and culminates in a delusional expectation of punishment" and, in his well-known phrase, said: "the shadow of the object fell upon the ego". John Byng-Hall (1973), in his work with families, adapted the aphorism and suggested that where there had been a death in the family "the image of the lost person can become resurrected in a remaining member of the family". It seems to me that the "remaining member" can then feel guilty about occupying the place of the lost person. She has, therefore, to limit her achievements and spoil her space both to assuage her guilt and also to guard against retribution from the dead person.

As a replacement child, she also seems to feel guilty about being alive at all and about the possibility of enjoying herself. She has to make her whole existence unbearable to prevent herself from being envied by the stillborn child. I realize that this is, of course, a problem for survivors of most disasters, such as those who have lived through the holocaust or survived a natural disaster or a man-made one, such as the Zeebrugge ferry tragedy.

Dr. Emanuel Lewis suggested that, following a stillbirth, it must be a problem for the mother to hold on to sufficient maternal preoccupation during her next pregnancy. Her whole body and mind have been centred on creating a whole, live, well baby. When she produces a dead one instead, it must be almost impossible for her to commit herself to the idea of a live child the second time round. Lewis writes:

> After a stillbirth there is a double sense of loss for the bereaved mother, who now has a void where there was evidently a fullness. Even with a live birth the mother feels a sense of loss, but the consolation of a surviving "outside baby" helps the mother to overcome her puzzling and bewildering sadness at losing her "inside baby". With stillbirth the mother has to cope with an outer as well as an inner void. [Lewis & Page, 1978]

The subsequent child feels responsible for the death and damage to the sibling. She appears to imagine that they shared the womb together, and that the dead baby was killed by getting out first (leading the way into the dangerous world while she hung back in the safety of the mother's womb).

The live children I see, who have been preceded by a stillbirth, imagine death as the envied state. It means returning to Mother Earth and metaphorically to the womb, so the child feels that by being alive she has been pushed out and rejected. Her desire to get back inside is demonstrated by her intrusiveness.

This then is her dilemma. She imagines that the idealized, beloved, dead baby is living inside her mother's body, and so she wants to be back there, too. On the other hand she feels anxious about the contents of her mother's body because it is seen to be damaged, and exploration is therefore frightening.

If we look at the Kleinian view that the unconscious regards the mother's body as the container of all marvels and all knowledge, and conversely that the woman's body can also be dreaded as a place of destruction, then, as Melanie Klein says, this could be a basic factor in inhibiting the desire for knowledge. She writes:

> It is essential for a favourable development of the desire for knowledge that the mother's body should be felt to be well and unharmed. It represents in the unconscious the treasure-house of everything desirable which can only be got from there, therefore, if it is not destroyed, not so much in danger and therefore not so dangerous itself, the wish to take food for the mind from it can more easily be carried out. [Klein, 1931]

I imagine, therefore, that if the mother's body is proved to be a "place full of destruction" because it produces stillborn infants rather than live, healthy ones; or if it appears too fragile to withstand fantasied attacks from other unborn or born siblings, or the unborn foetus, then the wish to take in food for the mind must surely be imbued with all sorts of dreads and inhibitions.

I will reiterate: the replacement child feels guilt about occupying the place of the dead child, so she has to limit her achievements and spoil her space both to assuage her guilt and also to guard against retribution from the dead person. She feels envy because of the idealized and loved place the dead baby holds in her mother's mind and (in fantasy) in her body. She feels hatred and sadistic murderousness because she imagines she has killed off the dead baby and is still killing off non-existent subsequent ones.

She also feels rejected because she has been pushed out of her mother's mind and body by the beloved dead infant.

Vincent Van Gogh was born exactly a year after the death of his stillborn brother, who was also named Vincent. Nagera (1967), in his psychoanalytic study of Van Gogh, explores in detail the effect of being the subsequent child after a stillbirth. He writes:

> The brother, being stillborn, had never had an identity of his own in reality, but for this very reason an ideal one had been created in the fantasy life of the parents. He would have been the perfect child, the compendium of all virtue, ability and kindness. He would always have done everything right and, especially where Vincent failed, the other, the dead Vincent, would have been successful. This extreme degree of idealisation of a dead child explains the high ego-ideals which the live Vincent set himself, his dread of failing and his fear of success. Against such high ego-ideals he would, of course, nearly always fall short. [Van Gogh, 1979]

And as we all know, Van Gogh committed suicide only a few months after the birth of another Vincent, his brother Theo's child.

Case illustration

I would like now to examine in detail my work with a child who was born after a stillbirth. She is also the youngest child in the family, which I think is relevant because there have been no live babies after her.

Jackie was twelve years old, the youngest child in a large family and lived at home with her father, mother, and elder sister. A baby girl died at birth between two of her older siblings. However, at the assessment interview this was described briefly as a miscarriage, and was not discussed further. Jackie was referred to the clinic because of her severe learning difficulties and her immaturity, although she was of average intelligence with no specific weakness other than a slight hearing loss. At the family interview it seemed clear that it was in the parents' interest to preserve Jackie as the handicapped baby of the family. They emphasized that she had fallen out of her cot and hit her head on a radiator when she was a young baby, and she was also described by her mother as accident-prone and uninterested in taking care of herself. It was suggested by a psychiatric social worker at the assessment interview that perhaps Jackie's apparent stupidity was a way of keeping the family together. Jackie seemed placidly to accept this role and to enjoy her powerful position of babyhood. She did not score on any reading test, and was apparently unable to remember any word for longer than thirty seconds.

She was a short, overweight child, with darkish wavy hair, blue eyes, buck teeth, and an appealing, friendly smile. When I first met her she made me feel as if she was a plump, jolly baby, bouncing winsomely and determinedly in her pram, who obstinately refused to make any move towards adulthood. This idea was exacerbated by the way she dressed, which was reminiscent of a fat toddler. She would often appear in baby-pink long-johns, white socks, a white vest, and a white hip-length broderie anglaise grubby petticoat. At the end of her mother's bed, a life-size doll was kept, dressed in Jackie's broderie anglaise christening clothes.

I constantly discussed, with Jackie, some of her reasons and wishes to remain a baby, and she began to make some move towards learning and towards realizing that it was her decision not to read.

However, my strongest feeling about her was one of murderous-ness. I felt intensely that she was constantly destroying anything creative that might be happening between us. She was provocative and stubborn about learning, and I would often feel consumed by a desire to shake her until she was dead. She would sit picking at the side of her mouth until she was disfigured by a red, raw spot, and she would wring her hands and mock-wash them like Lady Macbeth.

I would now like to describe part of a session with Jackie when she was trying to read from the Fuzz-Buzz (a reading scheme that uses a mainly phonic approach with constant repetition of the same words). It is about the adventures of some little creatures known as the Fuzz Buzz.

I must remind you that she was twelve years old.

"Ooh, Goodie, Macfuzz". Jackie puffed out her chest and clapped her hands. She opened the book and looked at a picture of a river running down a hill.

"Ooooh, it's a weeny weeny lickle river up there" she exclaimed.

"Do you have another way of saying weeny weeny?" Long pause—Jackie stuck out her bottom lip and looked sulky: "small" she said "a small river".

"Good", I replied: "Quite right". She began to read. She stopped at the word "first" and read "at the moment". "The river is small at the moment".

I said "Good, you obviously understand what you are reading, but that word doesn't say 'moment', it says 'at f-...'. What word means 'at the moment' but begins 'f? 'The river was little at f.-..?' "

"At figgy. The river was little at figgy. That's what it is."

"Jackie, you're destroying the meaning. I know you know the word. You're just showing me you want to stay a non-reading baby. You don't want to be a growing-up twelve-year-old."

"I don't know it. I don't ... I don't. At Fred—at fink." Jackie stamped.

"It reminds me of the time when you wouldn't read the word 'letter'. You kept saying the postman delivers parcels, envelopes, stamps, everything except letters."

"I didn't know 'letters' and I don't know 'first'." Jackie pouted—stuck out her bottom lip and read furiously "The river was little at first."

Her imaginative play at this time suggested that she was very concerned about other members of the family. She seemed to feel that there were murderous feelings towards herself and from herself towards her parents and also between her parents. She felt she was in the way—a perpetual nuisance.

Van Gogh mentions similar feelings in a letter to his brother Theo in 1884:

"I feel what father and mother think of me instinctively (I do not say intelligently)…. They feel the same dread of taking me in the house as they would about taking a big rough dog. He would run into the room with wet paws—and he is so rough. *He will be in everybody's way.*". (My italics) "And he barks so loud. In short, he is a foul beast." [Van Gogh, 1979]

She also appeared to feel anxious about growing up. Age was synonymous with infirmity.

There was also a sadistic quality in the counter-transference she aroused in me. She constantly made me feel that she was destroying what we were trying to create between us. She would walk into my room with a mixture of a waddle and a bounce, nose in the air, sit down over-purposefully, give a little wriggle, clap her hands, open her book, squeal: "I know it" and say something like,

"Sugar under cover is yellow jam"—what was written was "Shorty started to bark."

On these occasions I took to saying nothing. Jackie would continue: "That's right—I know it is. Oh no, 'Shorty ... um ... um ... started ... to ... laugh' ... oh no ... dogs don't laugh ... ha-ha ha ... 'bark' that's it ... 'Shorty started to bark'."

By the end of her first term with me I thought Jackie was afraid to progress. There was disaster in every step forward that she took. She appeared to be firmly convinced that success spelt pain and trauma, so it was better to remain a non-reading or non-learning child. She was frightened of failure and also terrified of success.

A year after I had started seeing her I felt that, although her ability to decipher words had improved, she was sadistically enjoying making rubbish of the text by misreading to such an extent that the result was nonsensical; for example, "For the rest of the afternoon" became "For the ready of the apinoog."

I suggested then that she rubbished her handwriting, her reading, and her speech in the same way. She turned everything that she did into a meaningless mess so that she could not be envied for being alive. I made this comment without being aware of the stillbirth.

When she came to see me after her mother had been ill, I suggested that she must have been very worried when her mother was in hospital. She said: "Yes, there's been lots of deaths in our family. My mum's kid sister died of cancer, and her father two years after I was born, and she had a baby between Peter and Patsy that died."

I asked her to tell me about the baby and she said:

Oh, it was born with half a face; it was in them old-fashioned days, and my mum smothered it with a pillow—murder it was, I suppose. Sometimes I think the baby's angry with me because I've got the baby's bedroom you see, and it comes into my bedroom and messes it up and spoils it. The baby was called Patsy, and that makes Patsy very angry, you know. She'd've been called Jackie and me, I don't know what I would've been called. Perhaps I wouldn't've been there.

At this point I began to understand that Jackie felt haunted by the feeling that she had replaced the dead baby (dead handicapped baby?) and that she must not allow life to be too perfect for her.

The feeling that Jackie was haunted continued, and also the fact that she could invoke murderous anger, which seemed to be connected with her feeling that she had murdered her mother's babies, or had wished to do so. At the beginning of a term she misread "elbow" in spite of context and picture clues. She read it as "eggwag" and thus made nonsense of the text. I, in my beginning-of-term, non-therapeutic vein, said: "Jackie, stop it or I'll strangle you."

She looked very alarmed, and said: "Oh, sorry, elbow".

Later during the same session I was struck by two of her miscues. "Until you find me" became "under my feet", and "hug" became "gun"; I wondered to myself whether she felt that her mother actively disliked her and would like to get rid of her, and also whether she felt she wanted to murder what her mother had made.

Meanwhile the haunting continued. During her last session of that term she described her adventure of the previous evening, when she was in a friend's house with three other girls, including her sister. When they were answering the telephone in the kitchen they heard a scream and a mug fell to the floor, which the girls decided was due to a ghost. I asked Jackie who she thought the ghost was. "Not the dead baby", she replied aggressively and somewhat melodramatically. "Well, whose?" I enquired. "I don't know, but it needs forty dogs and a vicar to get rid of."

I wondered to myself whether she was telling me that her ghost was one that was going to be particularly hard to exorcise, and maybe she did not want to get rid of it anyway?

A year later, Jackie reinforced the impression that she wanted to hang on to her neurosis at all costs. She misread the word "indeed" as "in baby". When we started to explore this she drew a picture of her mother's bedroom. At the end of the double bed was a rocking chair and in it a life-size doll dressed apparently in Jackie's christening robes. I wondered with Jackie what the doll made her feel. "Sad", she said: "But my mum likes talking to it and it cheers her up". I discovered from the psychiatric social worker, who visited the family at home, that this was true.

Later that week she drew a picture of a baby girl ghost, which she agreed was her little, dead sister. "I like it. It's not a frightening ghost—I want to keep it forever". When she told me this I felt she was trying to let me know how angry and despairing she felt with her mother for hanging on to the idealized plastic image of the dead baby. There was nothing she could do to alter her mother's stubborn insistence on hugging this dummy to her.

A few weeks before I finally said goodbye to Jackie she demonstrated her wish to intrude into the dead baby's space.

"I always dream the same dream. I dream a murderer's chasing me, and my friends tell me to jump off a cliff because he's chasing me." "That doesn't seem very helpful of your friends", I commented. "Oh, well, it's only a little cliff. There's a lot of little cliffs where I live." "In Hackney?" "Well, you know what I mean. It's quite safe to jump over them." "I'm wondering why the murderer wanted to murder you." "Well, I invaded her private property." "Her?" "Him, I mean—I invaded his private property. I ran along this half-bridge which is broken at the end. It goes over some water and I jumped into the private property. Look, I'll draw it". And she did so. I commented: "It looks to me as though you've missed the private property and you're going to fall into the water. Perhaps that's why you keep having accidents." "No" said Jackie: "It's all right, I get into it. Really there's no-one in it, but the murderer thinks it's hers." "She's an awfully small murderer", I said: "She looks a bit like a baby to me—a baby murderer." "Oh here, I'll change it" said Jackie very anxiously. I said: "It's O.K. I think I understand what you're getting at."

Jackie quietly returned to the book, reading avidly with no mistakes, apart from misreading "strange" as "strangle". She finished her session by asking if she could paint the clay cradle she had begun the week before, saying she wanted to paint it white on the outside and bright red inside: "I think I'll paint the baby black" she added: "No, no, I mean white." As she jabbed her brush viciously into the cradle I observed a mixture of emotions on her face. The pouting, trembling lip of the rejected toddler who feels ousted by the intrusion of a baby into her life, combined with an intensely loving gratitude and possessiveness.

Discussion

It seemed to me that Jackie needed to punish herself for her intrusive wishes and the damage she felt she had caused both to the baby and her mother. To return to Melanie Klein's idea, since Jackie felt responsible for damaging her mother's body she was unable to learn, both because she felt responsible and guilty for the damage she had inflicted and also because she felt afraid to take in knowledge from this damaged interior. She had within the last four months been knocked down by a car, fractured her ankle, had her tonsils out, fallen off the ropes in the adventure playground, slipped over in the mud, cut her knees on the way to the clinic, and cut her heel on the way to the clinic. Her escort described her crossing the road in front of her. "When the lights are green she starts to cross but doesn't go in a straight line. She wobbles towards the traffic almost as though she wants to get run over."

As well as wishing to punish herself, did Jackie also feel that the only way her mother, and I in place of the mother, would appreciate her was if she remained handicapped in some way?

Her ambivalence towards her mother was her predicament. She loved her mother dearly, her mother had brought her alive into the world, had materially cared for her and was continuing to care for her. On the other hand, she hated her for her preoccupation with the dead baby, for allowing the baby to die (although, as Jackie herself said, she, Jackie, might not be alive if the baby had lived), for her failure to mourn the death, and for her mother's eternal reverie with a dead object.

Salvador Dali, who was born after the death of his elder brother, also named Salvador, describes a similar experience (Unspeakable Confessions, 1976):

I lived through my death before living my life. At the age of seven my brother died of meningitis, three years before I was born. This shook my mother to the very depths of her being. This brother's precociousness, his genius, his grace, his handsomeness were to her so many delights, his disappearance was a terrible shock. She was never to get over it. My parents' despair was assuaged only by my own birth, but their misfortune penetrated every cell of their bodies and within my mother's womb I could already feel their angst. My foetus swam in an infernal placenta. Their anxiety never left me. Many are the times I have relived the life and death of this elder brother whose traces were everywhere. I feel he was a kind of test-run of myself.

Jackie's fear of being unable to match a dead ideal, her sadistic destructiveness of what she and I created, particularly the written word, and her guilt about living in someone else's shoes all contributed to her difficulties with learning.

CHAPTER SEVEN

A boy who used numbers as a defence against feelings

Heather Geddes

S tan was seven to eight years old and in Year 4. He was under-achieving, a reluctant reader and writer, and subject to violent outbursts in response to slight triggers, which disrupted the class and his learning. The primary concern was his behaviour.

He was a small, lean boy with a light bald patch that gleamed through his dark hair—caused by him pulling at his hair on the right side. He was observed around the school, walking about with his head lowered and with a more or less permanent glum expression of "it's not fair" on his face. He was frequently involved in incidents of fighting and hurting others in the playground, always saying it was someone else's fault. Stan's father complained that Stan was being bullied at school, which was why he had left his previous primary school and been relocated. At times the incidents were serious and in response to the slightest provocation. His unpredictable and reactive behaviour was clearly a concern and, with his father's permission, he was referred for educational psychotherapy with a view to helping him to express his anger and other feelings more appropriately and to address any emotional blocks in his learning. It was agreed that I would work with him in school.

Stan's family history was known to his school. He had been living with his mother, other siblings, and mother's partner, during which time there had been considerable domestic violence between the couple and towards Stan. This was investigated by Social ervices and it was decided that Stan and his sister would live with their father. The mother chose to remain with her partner. Stan saw his mother fortnightly at supervised access visits. It was reported that at times, during violent incidents between his mother and her partner, Stan had hidden behind the sofa with a calculator, doing sums. This helped to make sense of much of his later behaviour.

Stan's father was the family contact. He was a sensitive man and very concerned about Stan's behaviour in school, but saw his episodes of aggressive behaviour as an outcome of bullying and not as expressions of Stan's experiences or feelings. His main concern was that Stan often fought with his sister, making their family life very difficult. He reported recent incidents of Stan smearing faeces on the bathroom wall and wondered if this was a reflection of Stan's lack of co-ordination and difficulties in wiping his own bottom. Although concerned, he seemed very disappointed in Stan and there seemed little communication or trust between them.

We arranged to meet for four sessions initially. Stan was pleased with the plan to have individual time and came willingly to his first assessment session. He sat on a cushion on the floor. He made some eye contact and smiled from that position but said little and expressed little curiosity. I had a strong sense of his feeling "little" and vulnerable. He responded to being asked to share a task at the table and his first drawing was of a figure of a person. He drew Dennis the Menace (the very naughty character from the Beano comic) in bold red and black. He said he liked Dennis because of his dog Gnasher, a fierce little creature who was not drawn in the picture. There was a sense that Dennis had a fierce side that was kept apart, perhaps like Stan. Dennis was well but very awkwardly drawn with the left hand. The Dennis figure showed careful detail, but the right and left sides were out of proportion, with the right side arm and leg bigger than the left side, and the right eye smaller than the left, giving Dennis a slightly lopsided look. This made me think of his very awkward left-handed management of his pencil and his father's comments about co-ordination. The writing that accompanied the picture was, however, very well spaced and neat in chunky letters, but by his name there were two letters like Bs with crosses through them. This suggested to me that there were other bits that could not be expressed or had to be left out.

I asked about the rest of his family and Stan went on to describe them, denying any knowledge of where his mother lived or with whom. Instead he complained about his sister swearing at him and listed his aunts, uncles, and cousins, counting them on his fingers. He recited their birthdays and ages. His mother was conspicuously left out. I asked him to help me to make a date line of his life history and he described how his mother and father split up when he was five years old. He read "Not Now Bernard" and told me it had been his favourite book since he was five years old. He chose a picture of Bernard turning into a monster as his favourite.

I wondered aloud about the boy in the story who was angry with his mother for being too busy to notice him. He then went over to the sand-box and acted out a battle in the sand between his soldiers and mine in which mine were all vanquished and thrown out. He suddenly needed to go to the toilet and I was reminded of his father's concerns about Stan smearing faeces. I wondered about the psychological meaning of this sudden need to evacuate something from his body.

Perhaps my interpretation about a boy's anger towards a mother, who did not notice his distress, had stirred up overwhelming feelings he urgently wanted to be rid of. Beating me in the battle in the sand may have symbolized, in his internal world, a violent attack on a mother towards whom he felt intense rage and this may have aroused a fear of his having inflicted harm on me/her. His play in the sand may also have had some connection with earlier aggressive fantasies involved in his smearing faeces (see Chapter Two, discussion on internal world and, for example, the case illustration of Roger).

When he returned he wanted to play Snakes and Ladders, as if needing the certainty of a game with rules and structure following the arousal of powerfully destructive feelings for which he felt the need of a safely controlled outlet.

Stan chose the doll's house in the next session and filled it with a large family with "not enough room" and with a "mad boy" on the roof. But "mad boy" fell into the road and was run over by a police car. He grinned gleefully. I wondered (to myself?) about who "mad boy" might be and whether he had been excluded from the house for being the "mad" and dangerous person who had harmed Stan and his mother and who was harmed in turn by the police. It was as if Stan's rage towards his mother's partner was being vividly communicated in his play. The "kind" father then took charge and made food for all of them. This seemed like a narrative of his experiences of his family and their relationships, his rage at the person who had caused his exclusion from his mother's family and then the reconstitution of a family with his father.

In further sessions, he showed great reluctance to let me set any task. This suggested a lack of trust and a need to be in control. I thought that related to a preoccupation with unresolved and unprocessed experience, which inhibited his self-expression and blocked his thinking. He ignored my choice of books and took out "Where's Wally?" intently searching the pages as if I was not there. He returned to his play in the dolls house, arranging the family sitting on the sofa watching TV and being fed. Then, after drawing two fishes fighting under water, he returned again to board games and defeated me by changing the rules and ignoring "the truth". It seemed as if any foray into feelings and self-expression had to be limited and controlled by certainties and structure, as if he felt he could regulate his feelings in that way.

The end of the initial assessment coincided with the Christmas break. Before leaving, Stan stood in the box of sand and crouched down. It seemed a poignant moment and I commented on his wish to stay in the room and for us to go on playing and talking together. At the review meeting with his father, it was agreed that the sessions would continue. His father seemed more able to acknowledge that past experiences may have affected Stan. He remembered that Stan had actually been able to count before he talked and he recalled again how Stan had hidden behind the sofa doing sums on his calculator. We talked of him as counting rather than feeling and discussed that talking together was important.

I felt that Stan's main psychological problems had been revealed in his play and that this set the agenda for our work together. His preoccupations seemed to concern his absent mother, his feelings about her choice to stay with her abusive partner rather than with him, and also the traumatic experiences of domestic violence, with associated fears and helplessness, against which he had to defend himself psychologically. I viewed his lack of trust, need to take control, and reluctance to explore emotional states as direct outcomes of his experiences, affecting his capacities to engage in creative activities with words and drawings. His inhibited learning may also have reflected very primitive anxieties about "knowing" and "finding out" about his mother's body and its contents, affected by fears about his mother's body violated by actual violence and the fantasied effects of his own rage (Barrows, 1984).

Fear of dependency can exacerbate underachievement because of the fear of dependence on the teacher for support when challenged by learning. Bick (1968) describes how the

> Primitive fear of the state of un-integration underlies the fear of being dependent; that to experience infantile feelings of helplessness, brings back echoes of that very early unheld precariousness and this in turn motivates the patient to hold himself together ... a further block to emotional development.

In defence against this precariousness, Stan may have resorted to the certainty and predictability of numbers and concrete activities to keep his overwhelming and flooding feelings at bay.

He returned after the Christmas holidays with a more conspicuous bald patch and I wondered about the tensions of family life in the "festive" period. He described many relatives, and again gave their ages and birthdays and I wondered if he thought about numbers in order to feel safe. He said "Yes" but in response to my request to draw a house, he began to draw a box, like a frame, and filled it up with the markings of a football pitch.

The drawing made me feel suddenly numb and unable to understand his feelings or the meaning of the content, perhaps a countertransference experience of Stan's need to numb his feelings about a family festivity in which he was displaced from his mother.

I said it was hard to understand what his drawing meant and I felt left out. He smiled gleefully as if enjoying my confusion. He continued to draw and I described what he drew, the football sides who played against each other, with an umpire who kept the rules and made it safe. I wondered, aloud, if this drawing expressed Stan's experience of living in two families which were separated and opposed. Perhaps the central spot represented himself, caught in the conflict between keeping them apart and holding them together. I wondered to myself how he felt about his mother staying with the abusing partner in preference to him. I also wondered about his possible feelings of being excluded and left out of his mother's presence and how much this resentment and anger may have been acted out in the family he shared with his father. His aggression towards his sister was perhaps displaced anger felt towards his mother, but not acknowledged. It was possible to imagine considerable conflict between the two families and the children caught between. Stan resisted any attempt to explore the feelings associated with this separation, but I no longer felt unable to think. I was aware of Stan's inhibiting stuckness.

He was trapped in conflict and unable to write or explore uncertainty because his learning and thinking were impaired by the repression of hostility related to unprocessed traumatic violence. Perhaps he feared his pen was a destructive weapon rather than a safe tool for expression (Klein, 1931). I was aware of being the observer, paying attention to every detail of behaviour and sensitive to the emotional content of what was communicated—waiting to see what unfolded rather that initiating action (Salzberger-Wittenberg et al., 1983/1993).

The football game became the chosen metaphor. Each session then included a re-enactment of a game of two opposing teams. Stan ignored any task set and proceeded to set up the room as a football pitch, with him attacking the goal with a soft sponge ball and myself as the goalkeeper. He scored triumphantly. I was often aware of his hostility and glee as if some sadistic gratification accrued from having the power to hurt and control me and I found myself thinking that, thankfully, the sponge ball was relatively harmless. I think the fact that he knew it was not going to harm me in reality and the structure of the game, which provided some limits and containment, meant he felt free to express his aggression towards me in a safe way.

The game became very repetitive, however, and I despaired after some weeks about the possibility of it ever becoming any different. I put my feeling of being stuck into words and talked about how hard it was to think and how I felt as if he wanted to hurt me at times. I wondered aloud if he might be angry about something or someone who might have hurt him. The game then gradually changed. The activity shifted from a focus on attacking "the goalie" and, over the next few weeks, another player entered the game, a player who "fouled" him in the penalty area. The player "broke the rules", "hurt him" and was given first a warning yellow card and eventually, after several incidents, he was given a red card and told he could not play again. I interpreted this behaviour in terms of a player who hurt and frightened him and who was told not to return so that the game could be played fairly and the players could be kept safe. This felt a significant communication and perhaps marked the beginnings of possible integration. First Stan put his experience into actions, symbolically, in the game, in a way that I could understand and think about and put into words, making my thoughts available to Stan. As Boston and Szur stated

> It makes a great deal more sense of the seemingly unreasonable or outrageous behaviour of many children, if one bears in mind that they are often doing to others what they experienced as having been done to them, both internally and externally. [Boston and Szur, 1983, p. 3]

In such cases memories do not remain in the past, but become actions in the here and now. In a later session, when Stan had been hurt in the playground, he came sobbing to the session saying his legs had been "stamped on" and later that his face had been "squeezed"—he showed me how, gripping his face with his hand. (An incident of his face being squeezed and his nose bitten had led to Social Services involvement and precipitated his removal from his mother's house.) I wondered if he was showing me how much he had been hurt and I felt at that moment that he was describing the actual hurts from the past and that these had at last been thought about, understood, and put into words.

There seemed to be two strands to our "agenda", the gradual processing of past traumatic violence and the context in which he experienced the fear and violence—his parental relationships. I found myself wondering about his feelings towards a mother who did not protect him, with whom he might be very angry and disappointed, but whom he also longed to be with; a complex relationship in which, to be close to her risked violence and hurt, but to be apart implied a sad longing. This is the dilemma of a primary relationship in which the secure base is unavailable at times of greatest need. Characteristically, this leads to the disorganized attachment pattern described by Main and Solomon (1986) with its implications for behaviour and learning (Geddes, H. 2006a; Chapter One of this book).

As the references to violence and hurt in his play receded, Stan's confused and angry feelings became more directly evident in the transference and in his actions in the sessions. Resolving these feelings was complicated by the fortnightly visits with his mother, which seemed to trigger further bouts of rage and disappointment. In review meetings at school his teacher commented that his behaviour was more unreliable after these visits. The beginnings of the sessions were marked by Stan running to the room ahead of me so that when I opened the door he was waiting for me to find him. He would grin gleefully as I walked into the room. Was this his pleasure at the repeated certainty of our reunion or another version of his control over our union?

Over time, Stan began to respond to tasks introduced by me into the sessions, making use of the metaphorical potential. It was as if his capacities to feel and to think were becoming more available to him and he became interested in stories. He became angry with me when the sand was not wet enough, imperiously reminding me that I must remember what he wanted.

I was able to comment on his disappointment when I did not get things right or understand just what he wanted. I was hurt "accidentally" when a dinosaur was thrust into the sand very near to my hand as we were arranging animals. It seemed as if Stan's focus had now shifted from the frozen state of unresolved trauma to pre-occupation with his ambivalent feelings about his mother, a mixture of longing and rage. His rage was gradually processed in the context of his play, acknowledged, and contained within the therapeutic relationship. Stan was then able to explore more hopeful expectations of a relationship. He used two puppets who were friends and who played together, having fun and arranging outings and helping each other. Could it be that Stan was able to make use of the substitute good relationship that was available, rather than perpetually harbouring his grievance and holding onto his perceived abandoning mother with such intensity?

He played with his angry feelings by placing the books about angry boys (such as "Angry Arthur", "Where the Wild Things Are",

"Ned and the Joybaloo", "The Bad Tempered Ladybird", "Naughty Nigel", and "I feel Angry") in a line and using them as skittles, hurling the sponge ball at them with joyful glee. This capacity to play with these ambivalent feelings seemed liberating and hopeful. Containment of strong and destructive feelings can lead to integration of feeling and thought and so liberate creativity.

I was aware, in the transference, of Stan's need to feel safe. I was strongly reminded of the importance, emphasized by Emanuel, of the role of the "containing other" in coping with adversity and of Bion's Theory of Thinking, linking the containment of anxiety with the development of the capacity to think. In my role, as container of his disappointment and rage, I experienced Stan's transferred rage with his mother, whom he had perhaps experienced as unavailable and un-attuned to his experiences of fear and vulnerability, leaving him exposed, vulnerable, and helpless (Emanuel, 2000; Bion, 1962b).

His Year 5 teacher reported that Stan was calmer in class. His bald patch was filling up with a luxurious growth of dark hair. He was able to use his "time out" card to withdraw when he was aroused, but was still prone to some reactivity when he had been on his fortnightly visit to his mother. He seemed disturbed by the event rather than reassured, which I had become aware of in the sessions. His teacher recognized his increased reactivity after his fortnightly contact visits with his mother and responded, not by exclusion and punishment, but by giving him special responsibility for numbers in the classroom, for example, keeping scores and remembering and recording number information for her and the class. It was as if his capacity to control his reactivity by concrete number work became a positive intervention rather than an avoidance of feeling. He was attending a group, run by the school Mentor, for boys who were not safe enough to play outside at break times, as it was felt that they might endanger others. He responded well to the strategies in those sessions and was very proud when he was allowed to play outside again because he had shown that he could "control his angry feelings".

This collaboration between therapist, his mentor who ran the "angry" group, and his class teacher was important. The shared understanding and reflective collaboration seemed to enhance the effects of the therapeutic intervention. An experience of adults who could think together was perhaps strengthening the containing experience that had begun in his psychotherapy. He continued to develop in his capacity to use objects, words, and symbols in tasks and activities in the sessions. He wrote more spontaneously to record the outcome of games and note events. The gaps in the sessions caused by holidays began to have meaning. He wanted some reassurance that we would meet again after these breaks. We made a calendar, which served to record the dates and times of our sessions and he used this concrete tool well to make sense of any uncertainty about separations.

Some months before his birthday, his strongly opposed feelings about his mother intensified as he anticipated a great party in their contact time. In a game of Pairs, in which he was drawing matching pairs of pictures, his initial enthusiasm for thinking of objects that went together deteriorated into drawing pictures of playing cards with numbers on them, perhaps reflecting his anxiety about the anticipated union on his birthday. His feelings towards his mother were poignantly demonstrated in his play with the toy animals. He paired a baby frog with a bigger, mummy frog and buried the baby frog in the sand while I closed my eyes; then I had to hide the mummy frog in the sand while he hid his eyes. He then searched for them both, separating and reuniting them over and over again. I wondered aloud about his happy feelings about seeing his mother at his birthday party and when they met on Sundays. He then took up the toy lizard and made it squeak very loudly, close to my ears, then filled its mouth with sand and squirted it towards me as if spitting something out. I felt as if his longing and idealization of his mother was very close to his rage. These opposing feelings were repeated in the session when he was marking, on his calendar, his party date and the Sundays when he would be meeting his mother. He said he wanted to be with her "24 hours all the year". When I again commented on how much he wanted to be with her, he became angry again and the mummy kangaroo was thrown very near to my face. It was then possible to understand and to comment on how angry he was at his exclusion from her. It seemed very difficult to reconcile his longing with his rage.

Over the weeks preceding the party, the intensity of the apparently irreconcilable feelings about his mother began to diminish. The puppet friends returned and began to act out their own party in the sessions. They had cakes and presents and often fun.

I was given a puppet part and we made up stories of outings and activities, which all involved experiences of rewards and treats. He began a story about a group of children who get together and live in a large mansion and are happy all the time. A father who could drive safely entered his play and I felt a sense of relief that a mediating, safe presence could be permitted. The beginning of integration of these opposing feelings, triggered by his experience with his mother and re-experienced in the transference, was apparent when he drew a complex squiggle (a random scribbled line for me to make into a picture: Winnicott, 1971b). In the squiggle I could not see a picture, and he said with a smile that it was a way of "letting Heather know when he was cross with her". I felt like smiling too at this change in his capacity to name a feeling that had for so long dominated his unconscious, to name "crossness" with a smile, a very diminished feeling from the overwhelming and potentially damaging rage he had previously expressed.

It may have been that his repeated expression of his strong rage and longing, which I had acknowledged and expressed, had enabled some integration of such extreme feelings. He had arrived at the depressive position in which strong but opposing feelings can be tolerated (Klein, 1952/1963). I was aware, in the countertransference, of my anxious feelings preceding the birthday weekend and my worry that the party would be a disaster and that Stan would return devastated by disappointment. This was not the case and in the session following the party weekend he described a pleasant day in which many relatives took part.

His use of a pencil increased in fluency. He spontaneously drew a water pistol squirting and wrote the words, "Fun Day at school", to describe his eager anticipation of the event planned for the next day. It seemed possible to experience fun, albeit with a water pistol.

As my work in the school came to an end, it was necessary to say goodbye and we worked towards this, using the calendar that Stan had made in anticipation of his birthday. Numbers again became a tool for managing anxieties and Stan took charge of marking days and dates. He attempted to take further control by trying to leave sessions early and described his disappointment at having to miss interesting lessons, which he said he would rather be at. With the support of the class teacher it was possible to negotiate the sessions until the planned ending. We shared and acknowledged his sadness and in the final session he revisited books he had enjoyed; buried and found objects in the sand, stood in the sand box and, as he left, flung a small handful of sand towards me so that I could acknowledge his "crossness".

Stan's teacher had become very attuned to him and her affection for him appeared to grow as his remoteness and anger diminished. She reported his greater engagement in his work, less reactivity, and an increased capacity to use his number skills.

The ending sessions included a final review with his father, which was a very different experience from the earlier meetings. His father said he was pleased with him and understood him better, Stan was getting on with his sister, and he was very handsome. I was reminded by this comment that Stan had grown considerably, his hair was thick and he truly was a handsome boy. It seemed that his emotional integration was reflected in his physical growth and development as well as in his academic progress. The importance of his father's positive response lay in his father finding him a more lovable child, perhaps a reflection of Stan's diminished rage and increased sense of self, which permitted more communication and trust. It seemed that his father's affection and new-found closeness could be relied upon to sustain Stan further. He could now tolerate the separations from his mother by relying on the function of a father to be an alternative attachment figure who could facilitate further development; a father who could be the agent of further change.

Conclusion

Stan's experiences of violent abuse significantly affected his development, emotionally, physically, and cognitively. However, despite the overall importance of such a traumatic experience, the core aspect of his difficulties seemed to arise from the basic uncertainties and anxieties associated with his relationship with his mother. Within this relationship, he appeared to feel insufficiently protected from the exposure to unprotected violence, to have developed little capacity to cope with the uncertainties and fears inherent in such exposure and ultimately his personality had become organized by intolerable levels of stress. He responded to unbearable stress by resorting to concrete number functions as a means of self soothing by turning to left brain distractions from overwhelming feelings.

Stan has famous allies in the use of this function. Oliver Sacks (2001) describes a similar experience when, at an early age, he was sent to a boarding school where he was repeatedly caned by a sadistic headmaster. He describes how he first turned to numbers and then to science as a solace at school. Via an important relationship with an uncle, this developed into a particular fascination and obsession with the phenomena and facts of chemistry. Ultimately he became a very successful neurologist and writer. His description of his experiences adds to our appreciation of the role of left brain function in calming aroused states and demonstrates how concrete and structured tasks can become tools in the response to challenging and reactive behaviour resulting from failure of the child's coping and containing systems (Geddes, 2006).

The therapeutic processes, involving containment, transference, and reflecting back understanding of Stan's direct and indirect expression of his feelings in a way that had meaning for him, clearly began a process of change that liberated Stan's developmental and creative potential and enabled him to become engaged in learning. It cannot be over-emphasized, however, that the collaboration between the members of the immediate network of the school setting contributed to the possibilities of change, by strengthening the containing function around Stan and his challenging behaviour. Educational psychotherapy, in acknowledging the close relationship between social and emotional experience and learning, is well suited to the educational setting. It can make a significant contribution to the more effective functioning of identified vulnerable children, as well as the whole school system, to the benefit of all the children and those who work with them.

CHAPTER EIGHT

Family dynamics and the educational experience

Muriel Barrett

I n my role as a remedial teacher/Educational Psychotherapist at the Tavistock Clinic, (1973–1986), I saw children individually and in peer and family groups, the latter sometimes with colleagues. All the children were referred for either lack of basic skills, suspended learning (suddenly being unable to continue learning), or showing resistance to learning.

Unlike the established mode of family therapy, our work focussed on the family dynamic relating to, and often reflecting, the referred child's capacity and attitude to learning skills and tasks. The dynamic of family behaviour sometimes mirrored their referred child's learning problems, particularly in relation to communication. If there were hidden agendas words became, consciously or unconsciously, misinterpreted. Families sometimes revealed certain attributes similar to those of their child:

- an aggressive stance
- bored indifference
- low self-esteem
- poor temporal sense (e.g. about appointment times)

- defensive behaviour (blaming others)
- an unclear sense of themselves as "competent and active members of the outside world" (Heard & Barrett, 1977).

A crucial key to understanding any family interaction is our own understanding of what we are experiencing in the transference or countertransference (see Chapter Two). Observation offers insight into secure or insecure patterns of attachment behaviour seen in the interaction between family members. Encouraging them to express opinions and feelings about each other either enhances or inhibits their willingness to acknowledge the significance of family loss or transitions. The parents' experience of their own education may affect the extent of their co-operation with us by their choosing:

- limited acceptance of help for their child
- to include parental ongoing participation
- to be open to links being made between family interactive behaviour and a referred child's capacity to learn

Case illustrations

A family with limited basic skills

Two of Mr and Mrs Bell's three children, Bobby, aged ten and Mary, aged eight years, were referred by a local primary school headteacher, with whom we had ongoing contact. It was difficult to engage with this family. After three failed clinic appointments, the headteacher arranged a meeting for us with the parents at the school. We reached an agreement to work in their home. We visited twice to find them apparently out, although we noticed the children had placed two toys facing outwards in the window. We wrote to say we were sorry we had missed them and one of us would call next week. When I visited them alone, Mrs Bell greeted me warmly with her youngest daughter, aged almost three years, who at first hid behind her mother's skirt, but soon engaged me in play. Her mother sat by an open doorway and said her husband was not well, although I sensed that he was within listening distance. Mrs Bell told me they had difficulty in getting the children to go to school. She claimed that the man living above would not let them pass him each morning, waved his walking stick, and shouted and there was too much traffic for them to cross to the other side. At this point Mr Bell appeared and joined in the discussion, pouring out their many woes about this tenant; he kept them all awake at night so the children were often too tired to go to school and Josie could not speak. Josie then went to the fridge, took out a feeding bottle and fruit juice, gave them to her father and said, "bot bot". His response, I noted, was a caring one. I was puzzled as to why it had not occurred to either parent to accompany their children to school as they lived on income support and did not work. It later emerged that they only left the flat once a week to collect their money.

I took some drawing materials, books, and various games, to introduce these parents to some of the activities we would use with Bobby and Mary. At this point Josie picked up one of the books and brought it to me. I felt that this second gesture from the little girl provided me with an entrance into the family dynamic. I said my colleague Ms Brown and I would look forward to seeing them all after school next week. When we arrived the father was nowhere to be seen and no explanation was given for his absence. We reintroduced ourselves and suggested that my colleague would work in one corner with Bobby and Mary, while Mr and Mrs Bell talked with me in another. Once work began Mr Bell appeared. After some reading games the children chose to play snakes and ladders. Ms Brown and the children discussed feelings about success when someone went up a ladder, disappointment about slithering down a snake and frustration when the dice dictated a player's difficulty in getting started or becoming stuck. This discussion with the children was paralleled by my discussion with the parents. The mother acknowledged that she could not get on at school, her mother had sent her to a special school, "because all me brothers went there and Mum liked it". Housekeeping skills were beyond her when she first married, but she then told me, with obvious pride and pleasure as she looked at her husband, "He learned me". I felt they both went up a ladder. Mary occasionally joined her parents, to read to them, while Bobby was engaged in choosing a book. He chose a story about an ogre. Josie flitted from one group to another, or stood between them drinking from her bottle. After "work" the children were invited to draw. Josie rushed to a table, picked up some drawing paper and gave it to her two siblings; her parents laughed.

Over the next few weeks Mr Bell spoke more openly about their fear of the tenant above them. The banging we heard on one occasion was indeed alarming. Shortly afterwards, the police became involved when this tenant broke through the ceiling and Bobby was concussed by the falling debris. It subsequently emerged that Mr Bell was unable to cope with any authority figures, including Social Services, and revealed that even having to face the post office staff to collect their benefits was a major undertaking.

There were two turning points in working with this family. Ms Brown was talking about the spelling homework that their father had asked for, when she suddenly turned to me and the parents' group and asked "How do you spell houses?" Everyone laughed and this led to a discussion about "not knowing" and that it was all right for an adult to not know something (but not in the Bowlbian sense of a parent's denial of the loss of a family member: see the following example). Bobby and Mary began to enjoy school and Bobby made considerable progress, but the parents continued to be very anxious about the court proceedings that were taking place. Even though I liaised with the police, the housing department, the school, a paediatrician, and Social Services, the upstairs tenant was not found guilty. The police, in particular, said they could never understand why the Bells lost the case.

After we had discussed writing to obtain rehousing, Mr Bell announced one week that a friend had typed a letter for them. This surprising enterprise was matched by Mrs Bell, who agreed to take Josie to a nursery group as a way of allowing them regular contact with other mothers as well as stimulating Josie's speech. The whole family came to a follow-up meeting in the clinic. While the theme dominating the discussion was anxiety about money, Josie emerged from the play-house and handed her father a box of plastic money. They were amazed that their "baby" daughter who so rarely spoke had demonstrated her understanding of her parents' concerns.

Suspended learning

A family secret was revealed after a boy of twelve years suddenly stopped learning in school. I first met the Brown family, whose neat and tidy appearance and respectful manner seemed to offer an image of themselves as very reliable and respectable people. The school, which had referred their son John, described the Browns as co-operative and always interested in their son's education. His progress in his schoolwork had been consistent throughout his primary school and had continued, at first, in his secondary school until he became stuck and was unable to maintain his previous steady progress. He and his parents were very polite in answering any questions regarding their concerns, but then seemed uncertain in their manner. They expressed their puzzlement about John's lack of progress and said that neither they nor his teachers could understand this change in his attitude to schoolwork. During the interview it transpired that John had been complaining of head-aches, but no medical cause had been found for them. When we explored the difficult experience of the emotional and bodily changes at the beginning of adolescence, the mother became very quiet. We talked about John's earlier schooling and his preschool days. The father then revealed that when John started school his older brother died from a brain tumour at the age of twelve (John's age now). Mother wept silently when this event was recalled and admitted that this was the first time that they had spoken of their elder son's death to anyone outside the family. (An aunt and uncle had taken John to his first day at school.) "John started school and we just carried on as normal". After a moment of silence John looked at his parents and then at me and began to reveal his anxiety. He had been unable to concentrate on his schoolwork because, when he began to have headaches, he feared that he too might have a brain tumour and worried about how his parents would manage if he died. Had the carefully preserved family face of normality become a burden for all of them? John's courage, in speaking so openly about his greatest fear, appeared to offer a sense of relief to them all, now that this painful secret had been shared with a professional, a non-family member (see Bowlby, 1988a).

Resistant learning

With the noisy and rushed entry into the room of a family with three children, we were left standing while they argued about seating. Finally we all sat down. This well-dressed, well-educated family presented themselves as rather subdued, apart from the father, Mr Baxter, who made it very clear from the beginning that he was in charge. What was the shared front the family presented; "the family face" as we termed it? It seemed to be "Yes, we are all in control here" which we read as "Yes, we are all being controlled".

The dynamic of this family—two parents, two boys of twelve and ten (the younger referred for "failing" in school), and a girl of six— changed rapidly during the first interview. Mr Baxter had marched into the room, sat down before anyone else, and started to complain about the behaviour of his younger son. His wife found it very difficult to answer any of our questions and was often in tears. The referred boy, his older brother and younger sister sat very close together on a sofa. The younger boy mumbled his answers and I wondered out loud if it was often difficult for him to make himself heard in his family. While the two siblings drew pictures, Father jumped in and told us it was impossible for him to speak in front of his children. We noticed that there was no communication or eye contact between the parents. Reluctantly, the father agreed to a second meeting, when we offered the alternative that one of us would see the parents alone while the other saw the three children. After these simultaneous meetings, I learnt that the father had continued his acrimonious comments about his son in the parents' meeting, while the mother admitted that she spoilt her younger son because he was not doing well at school. In the other room, with me, the older boy drew a monster, heavily outlined in black, while the little girl drew a fairy princess. The middle child stood by the door and told a story about a boy in his class who was stealing from the sweet shop next to the school. Did I think this was fair? I felt quite nonplussed and remained silent for a few moments. Again, I wondered aloud whether he was talking about stealing time for himself in his family? Before he could answer, the older boy told me that he stole his parents' attention by stealing his younger brother's felt pens. The little girl said, "I scream". Before we returned to the room where the parents had been talking with my colleague I asked the children if they would like to tell their parents about what we had discovered in their time with me. All three said "Yes". On our return to the other room mother's reaction to our reported "discovery" was to smile. Father on the other hand was furious; he asked me how I dared to put words into his daughter's mouth. It was not possible to continue. This particular family dynamic was painful to be part of, as we were unable to find a way into a more open discussion about the father's anger, mother's sadness, and the referred boy's fear of speaking out.

Play and learning

The following example incorporates elements of:

- a child's lack of basic skills and anxious attachment pattern
- a mother's suspended learning
- a father's resistance to learning and
- the use of play to address emotional problems that formed barriers to learning

Two colleagues, a Senior Social Worker and a Senior Psychiatric Registrar, had worked with the Burch family for a year, focussing on the parents' marriage and their management of Peter, just seven years old. The work did not include an older son. Peter was then referred to an Educational Psychologist, by the school. He was described in school as showing "unmanageable behaviour, for example kicking and hitting teachers and peers and an inability to learn". The psychologist's report suggested that "Peter is highly distractible, immature, difficult to engage, wary and exhibiting little self-esteem", and recommended Educational Psychotherapy. When I was introduced to the family by the colleagues who had been working with them, Peter rushed towards his mother and was enveloped by her. I smiled at him and listened while Mrs Burch described their life at the time of Peter's birth, becoming upset as she did so. She accused her husband of choosing to work some distance away from the family, for several weeks at a time, for the first few years of their younger son's life. He occasionally returned home at weekends. I felt that this experience of the "loss" of her husband's support had not been resolved.

Both parents accepted the suggestion of Educational Psychotherapy for Peter. I suggested to them all that Peter and I could work next door, on the other side of a one-way screen. I explained that they would be able to watch us working together for a short period, and then we would rejoin them to discuss, all together, what Peter and I had been doing and making.

The rationale for this choice was twofold, first of all to give the parents an opportunity to observe their son, in the company of the therapists who had been working with them, with a view to understanding Peter's approach to tasks and how his behaviour inhibited his learning. The second reason was the team's concern about the relationship between mother and her younger son, which was regarded as over-close, or "symbiotic" (already discussed prior to my joining the team). My observations and description of interactions with Peter and his parents are solely from my point of view. (Between sessions we three team-members shared our feelings and thoughts about what had taken place.)

First impressions

I saw the mother as a good looking, very well groomed, extremely thin woman. I understood the considerable concern that her appearance had evoked in my co-therapists. She looked ill. The father was smartly dressed and clean-cut in appearance. Peter was a good-looking boy whose behaviour, during the first few weeks of my intervention, was either to cling to his mother, to shout loudly, or to dash around the room. The mother occasionally made eye contact, but the father appeared to be intent on ignoring me. He sometimes shouted at Peter, but rarely engaged in a dialogue with his wife. I felt he wanted to be in control of me, the new person, and to monopolize the two original team members.

The first session with the whole team

Peter's screaming protest made it impossible for us to contemplate using the one-way screen. He was quite unable to tolerate separation from his mother; he clung desperately to her like a very frightened infant. I recognized that his mother too felt unable to separate herself from Peter. His father's reaction was to become angry and despairing, saying the situation was "hopeless". We decided to discuss the dynamic quite openly and concluded that Peter and I would stay in this room while everyone else watched us work. I attempted to enlist Peter's help by inviting him to re-arrange the furniture so that we could place ourselves a little distance away. When he was finally persuaded by his father to sit on a small chair at a small table, I tried to engage him by explaining what we might do. He watched me in silence and did not respond to any of the material I offered him. Later he gave only a slight indication of interest, but he frequently made eye contact. I was all too aware of my own tension and felt under considerable pressure from working in front of two colleagues, with whom I had never worked before, and Peter's parents. I felt, too, under my own internal pressure to create a "working and playing space" within which Peter and I would be able to interact and learn. I made a simple statement to share my feelings with Peter; "I don't think we are finding it very easy to work with other people watching us". I did this to try to create a boundary between an Educational Psychotherapist/seven- year-old dyad, and the four other adults present in the room (Barrett & Trevitt, 1991; Winnicott, 1971a).

Peter responded to my wondering aloud, "How shall we begin?" by answering questions about his likes and dislikes, which I recorded in his book. He was then invited to write his name on his book and his box, which he achieved with considerable difficulty. He was unable to attempt his surname (the box and other materials for his exclusive use had been introduced to him when we first met). One of Peter's likes was fish. I wrote the initial letter "f" on a chalkboard and invited him to draw a fish. He drew one with an open mouth full of sabre-like teeth. Again I mused to myself, wondering out loud why the fish looked so angry. Peter responded by becoming very upset and seeking close proximity to his mother, who assuaged his anxiety by again enfolding her son in her arms. Mr Burch ignored his wife and son and remarked that now perhaps we could see how impossible it was to teach his son. "It's up to you to find a way to make him co-operate". I silently shared his disappointment. He then addressed me directly, "You'll never get anywhere like that you know". This was to be the first of many expressions of criticism, which I felt included some feelings of rivalry towards me "the teacher".

My prime concern was Peter. I said how sorry I was that he had become so upset and then asked him to help me move our table closer to his parents, in case he wanted to seek help from either of them. (I sensed that it was important to allow him some degree of control in regulating the distance between himself and his mother to alleviate his sense of panic when he felt he was being separated from her abruptly.) I then picked up some plasticene and offered a piece to Peter as a way of encouraging him to return to a shared space of play. While we were talking about what each of us was making, Mr Burch intervened saying that Peter had made a very good dinosaur at home and ordered him to make another one now. Peter left his chair and leaned into his mother, asking for help with his model. Once it was completed the father took it and "corrected" it. His son in turn made it into an elephant. The father then picked out an elephant from among a box of toy animals I had ready for Peter's use, stressed that it was an elephant, and directed his son to get this right because it was no longer a dinosaur! Peter made no protest, copied the elephant placed before him, leaving what he referred to as the dinosaur spikes on its back. He then became upset and claimed that it was all wrong. I suggested that as it was Peter's elephant it could be as he wanted it to be.

I told Peter that our time together was almost over for this week. His mother immediately suggested to him that he could make some more models with me next week, as she helped place his dinosaur model in his box and smiled at me for the first time. Peter expressed great concern over the safety of his model. One of my colleagues commented that perhaps he was wondering if we could take care of him. As everyone was preparing to leave, Mr Burch tried to engage me in conversation, asking where he could buy some plasticene like the clinic's and what I was going to give Peter for homework?

Follow-up discussion of team

After this session we realized that we had independently noticed a subtle change in Mrs Burch's behaviour. Her facial expressions and body movements indicated a different understanding of her role beyond that of the need to assuage her son's anxious attachment behaviour. I knew I was holding in mind a very frightened and anxious little boy. I shared, too, with my colleagues, my own feeling of being de-skilled, while being admonished by the father. We were all aware of the mother's silent watchfulness and how frightened and bewildered she seemed to be initially, very uncertain of her role in this new way of working with her son. Our discussion about the feelings of anger in the session led us to think that father's anger towards his wife was being displaced on to me the "teacher". One

member of the team was aware that, as part of the transference phenomenon, the Educational Psychotherapist had become, for the
father, the punitive schoolteacher from his own school days. The
most experienced member of the team felt she was representing an
attachment figure for the family and the team.

Continuation of work with child and family

The following week Peter entered the room first, went directly to his
box, and took out his model. He said it had been looked after quite
well but it was "a little bit bent". Early in this session I found myself
reacting to the feeling I had of pressure from the father, although
I silently maintained the belief that Peter needed to be able to play
and learn at a pre-school level, that is to regress, educationally
speaking, before he could move forward (Barrett & Trevitt, 1991).
The pressure prompted me to adopt a more didactic approach by
picking up the model elephant and saying, "shall we write down
"e" for elephant in your book?" Peter's reaction was one of panic
and retreat. He turned to his mother, who looked particularly fragile, but when I re-engaged Peter with an alphabet jigsaw puzzle, the
success of the activity was largely due to mother's intervention and
interest. She looked frequently at me for nonverbal approval until
Peter became fully engaged with me and suddenly picked out the
letter c and spontaneously said, "'c' is for car". He talked about racing cars and began to make a model of one. This activity was again
taken over by father, who quickly abandoned his attempt and
handed it back to his son saying, "Here, you do it". He then
addressed me directly, pointing out that he had purchased some
vastly superior plasticene in a well-known London store. This was
followed by another request for homework. While Peter struggled
with his model-making, mother reflected back to her son an earlier
comment I had made to him. When he expressed discontent with his
efforts she told him, "It's your model, therefore it can be any design
that you choose".

For several weeks Peter was often uncooperative, although he
seemed less stressed and upset. His father's criticism of me continued to be explicit. He made reference to a work colleague who had
had to remain an apprentice because he could not read, adding,
"I must remind you that Peter is due to transfer to his next school in

a year's time" (i.e., to move up from Infant's School to Junior School). It transpired that Mr Burch believed that every child had to be able to read Roald Dahl's book Charlie and the Chocolate Factory (a reading age of about nine to ten) before they could enter this school. If we failed, his son would also remain an apprentice. When father asked what techniques we would be using, one of my colleagues suggested that he regarded the Educational Psychotherapist as an apprentice, because she did not give homework and only provided modelling clay. The father's response to this comment gave an indication, for the first time, of a shift in his thinking, albeit an ambivalent one. He suggested that I could play a car game with Peter, but followed this immediately by announcing "Obviously you are fighting a losing battle".

During our team discussion we recalled that the family had been prepared, at the time of Peter's referral, for techniques of Educational Psychotherapy, including the use of creative materials.

The father's suggestion of a car game proved to be a turning point for Peter (and me). I think that for both these parents, too, it showed an acceptance of a different way of working. I acknowledged Mr Burch's excellent suggestion, and the activity revealed a creative side of Peter. Initially his mother and I helped, but he gradually showed some independent creative thinking while constructing a race-track. The words and numbers that were incorporated as learning activities were accepted by Peter as part of his game. When he asked if he could finish the game at home, he was clearly making a link between the clinic and his home and I wondered if he saw this as a solution to his father's request for homework. I had to refuse a request for help from Peter in constructing a race-track for the game because, as I said, I had no idea what a pit stop looked like. This admission of mine led to one from the father. While the mother, Peter and I were engaged in the racing car game, he told the other two team members about his own failure to learn, at about Peter's age, and the subsequent punishments he had received.

In our discussion afterwards, we wondered if Mr Burch had been unconsciously, or even consciously, taking in the experience, not only of observing his son engaged in activities with an empathic teacher, but also of seeing the changes in his wife's management of her interactions with Peter. Mrs Burch continued to assuage Peter's anxious feelings, but now, when he sought physical comfort perhaps not age-appropriate for a seven-year old, she gently moved him away from this too close proximity and encouraged him to explore. Bearing in mind that there had been an agreement that the use of the one-way screen could still be a way of helping Peter to develop a more independent self, we discussed its use for the penultimate session before a half-term break. Peter's protest was loud and long and the session was a painful one, exacerbated by the father's statement: "It's all up to you to find a way to interest him, otherwise he will just not co-operate". When Peter continued to protest by screaming and kicking the radiator, he was taken outside into the corridor by his father, who could clearly be heard shouting angrily. On their return mother wept silently. The team expressed their concern for Peter and his parents and made reference to the pressure we all seemed to be experiencing. We expressed our belief that Peter needed his own space to play, learn, and interact with his therapist and that he, too, must be feeling under considerable pressure, while five adults discussed his behaviour.

After this comment Peter removed himself from the adults, climbed onto a high windowsill, and started hurling down balls of plasticene, still shouting loudly. When neither of the parents made any move towards him, I lifted him down telling him I was sorry he was feeling so angry and that I was afraid he might fall. He slumped on the floor close to the wall, while my colleagues and Peter's parents discussed a possible plan of action. I sat on the floor too, made some plasticene balls, and engaged Peter in throwing and catching the balls. On a symbolic level the game signifies a willingness to hold and let go, to share with another; a game normally associated with the play of a much younger child. It begins, developmentally, at the stage when a baby begins to realise the difference between "me" and "not me", as described by Winnicott (1971a). Peter's clinging over-dependence on, and frequent resort to, physical contact with his mother showed that he had had difficulty in negotiating that developmental stage. Perhaps this had some connection with his mother's need to keep Peter close to her. She had felt insufficiently supported during Peter's infancy, when her husband was periodically away from home and her own anxiety about separation probably made it difficult for her to encourage Peter to enter into exploratory play. This would have inhibited his behaviour at a time when it would have been appropriate for him to begin to develop some independent action. He may thus have remained emotionally entangled with his mother and anxious about separation.

His protest in this session had begun when we talked about separating him from his mother by using the one-way screen, which meant she would be out of sight on the other side of it. His hurling of the plasticene balls, from a somewhat dangerous position, can be seen as a demonstration of how dangerous it felt to him to be separated from his mother. If she disappeared behind the screen he would be unable to see her or turn to her immediately to be held and comforted when he felt anxious. This aggressive outburst at the prospect of separation, coupled with his anxiety, also hinted that he may have feared that his aggressive feelings could harm his mother and felt he had to stay close to her to make sure she was unharmed. (In the very first session, when I commented that the fish he had drawn with big teeth looked angry, he became very upset and sought close proximity to his mother who held him closely.) In my intervention, as well as removing Peter physically from the danger of falling from the high windowsill, I communicated, in words, my understanding of his anger. In this way I offered him the psychological "holding", which Winnicott emphasizes as essential for the therapist to provide in order to support a child through painful stages of emotional growth. With this support and containment Peter was able to make the transition from hurling balls of plasticene, in an uncontrolled angry fashion from a dangerous height, to throwing and catching them, in a game, within the relationship with me. This helped him to recover his equilibrium and he was able to return to a state of being able to play (Winnicott, 1971a). Cognitively the game entailed several skills, for example counting an equal number of balls each when we created a competitive aspect to the interaction.

Mother's initiative

Meanwhile the parents were still engaged with the shared problem of control, until the mother's initiative solved the anxiety about the use of the one-way screen. She told Peter she needed to go to the toilet and when she returned she would meet him and me in the room next door on the other side of the screen. She added that then the father would be able to watch them working together. Peter looked up, showed his capacity to tolerate this brief separation, and continued playing with me until we could see and hear mother next door. He told his father, very firmly, to stay where he was and he and I joined mother.

Behind the screen we played the game of Pelmanism. (All the cards in a pack are laid face down. Taking turns, each player chooses two cards to turn over, keeping them if they are a matching pair, turning them back over and replacing them if not. The aim is to collect the biggest number of matching pairs and, to facilitate this, memorize the cards previously turned up and their positions.) Peter became very excited when he won, but denied that he was pleased to win. He then announced that next week it would be his father's turn to come behind the one way screen.

Parental learning

Peter's experience of seeing adults learning was important (Pelmanism was a new skill for mother). Also the adults' co-operation in finding a solution to the use of the one-way screen seemed to help him towards an acceptance of it. Over a period of several weeks we noted several changes in Mrs Burch. She became less and less silent and, as her resolve increased, she openly disagreed with her husband's opinions. She looked more attractive and her manner became animated. We felt that her early signs of openness to learning by quiet observation and listening led to a gradual change in her behaviour towards Peter and gave her the confidence to recognize a change in her relationship with her husband. We felt she had absorbed a new way of seeing herself in action with her son and her husband and that this was based on her understanding of the team's approach to each other. Early on in the teamwork reported here Mr Burch said, addressing me, "You realize you've joined a very exclusive club here". He frequently criticized the subsequent play element of my work with his son. His early stance of scepticism had shifted considerably towards the end of the first term, however, as he voiced his surprised discovery of "how much one can learn through play". He told us that he had participated in his older son's school project designed to help parents understand some new mathematical method and it had been fun. During Mr Burch's time behind the screen with me and his son, the rivalrous behaviour he showed towards his son for my attention became quite difficult. It took several weeks to enable him to allow his son to win any games we played. It became easier when I was able to put myself down with number games. (My numeracy skills are basic.) I gave Peter a numerical task to complete and his father launched into an account of his own problem-solving skills with numbers.

After another term's work, with both parents accepting their roles as active or observing participants, Peter had a second psychological assessment. It was agreed that he and I would continue our work together without Mr and Mrs Burch or the team. The parents no longer wished to continue working with the original team, but welcomed the idea of a joint meeting once a term, to discuss Peter's scholastic progress, unless they or the school asked for earlier meetings.

A few weeks before my final individual sessions with Peter, we all met to hear the following report from the educational psychologist who had assessed Peter previously: "Peter related to me in a friendly and direct manner, and approached each task in a quiet and composed way. It is reasonable to suppose that he can continue to progress rapidly". It was noted that his creative writing had not yet reached the potential level that the psychologist thought would soon be possible.

Comment

The fact that marital difficulties and parenting skills had been a focus of the work prior to my engagement with this family enabled Mr and Mrs Burch to focus on the learning difficulties of their son at this stage of the work. I believe they provided Peter with role models of how to learn. As a team we felt that, although the mother's physical and emotional health was a major concern to the team, her own childhood experience of an attachment figure had been of one who offered her a secure base. We thought her capacity for updating an internal working model, of herself interacting with an attachment-figure; put her in touch with an earlier experience of assuaged attachment. In the beginning, her behaviour towards us showed extreme anxiety during any period of interaction. Now that she herself was in the role of an attachment figure she seemed to recognize her own needs, which she could set aside in order to meet those of her son. Our hypothesis was that her capacity for updating had become suspended at the time of the birth of her second son, when her husband was unable to provide a facilitating environment for his family (Winnicott, 1960). We believed this contributed to her too close relationship with Peter. This mother's observational skills and her willingness to become open to a different way of interacting shifted the interplay of the family dynamic. Peter seemed able to update his internal working model of himself learning, himself with his mother and later himself with his father. Through his modified interaction with his parents he showed that he understood the changes in his parents' behaviour towards him and each other. This enhanced his belief in his capacity to learn. The validation of his worth by the team also supported his ability to separate from his mother and "become his own person", a phrase used by Mr Burch. The father's behaviour seemed less responsive and open to change and when he brought Peter to his individual sessions at the clinic his behaviour was, at times, intrusive. On arrival he tried to enter the room in which Peter and I were working and he attempted to engage me in discussion at the end of each session, often seeking my advice about a problem he had. He then brought small gifts of chocolate and this reminded me of the pressure I had previously experienced from him in the early days of the work. Had I become an attachment figure who needed to be pleased or had I become a "good" teacher, no longer an apprentice? By my firmly maintaining a professional boundary, I felt Mr Burch, too, was able to separate from this relationship and explore his new life. This seemed very much in evidence at the end of my last session with Peter. Both his parents collected him. I was struck by the mother's attractive, healthy appearance and by how relaxed the parents were in each other's company. Peter greeted them with a smile and they all entered into an animated discussion about a forthcoming outing.

Although some families are resistant to new experiences, I think that any intervention into family dynamics is likely to bring about some change. In families who are secure in their attachments, losses will be managed in a way that enables the family, and the individual members within it, to mourn, express anger, sadness or joy, and to play, explore, learn, and continue their goal-seeking. For those whose experience has led to anxious attachments, a new way of playing and learning may be dismissed or only partially tolerated.

While maintaining homeostasis may feel safer for parents, I have found that many children recognize and readily respond to the idea of this new way of learning that is being proposed.

Editor's note:

The dynamics of the Burch family fit one of the patterns, identified by Irene Caspari, of a complex triangular relationship, with an over close tie between mother and son, in which both parents have unconscious reasons to feel threatened by their son learning to read and growing up (Caspari, 1986; Chapter Ten).

PART III

APPLICATIONS OF EDUCATIONAL PSYCHOTHERAPY

CHAPTER NINE

Therapeutic story groups: educational psychotherapy in a school setting

Gill Morton

The principles of educational psychotherapy can be a foundation stone for a medium term intervention in a normal school setting, offering a training opportunity for staff working with troubled and troubling children and, at the same time, offering a group of children a therapeutic opportunity, which can promote change. In the work I am going to describe, a collaborative narrative method is used. Group activities also allow for individual expression work, enabling the facilitating adults to pick up and talk in a safe way about the difficult feelings expressed in the imaginative material.

Children needing help in the school setting

Many children show signs of disturbance in class, in the play ground, at home-time when parents collect them, or at the beginning of the day when separating from home. Depressed, inhibited children make teachers uncomfortable; while noisy, disruptive, violent children may make them desperate. Many children who evoke such concern or irritation have difficulties in thinking. This does not necessarily mean a cognitive deficit or a "syndrome" such as attention deficit hyperactivity disorder (ADHD), dyslexia, or Aspergers Syndrome, although there may be elements of these broad areas of difficulty. The children I will be referring to can find it hard to think about the world they live in and may also have difficulty in thinking about themselves in relation to others. They will find it hard to manage being taught or to accept being given good educational food.

Resilience, learning, and the challenge of school

The works of Klein, Winnicott, Bowlby, and Bion have thrown much light on the links between anxiety experienced in infancy and early childhood, a lack of emotional holding at a crucial stage of development, and later difficulties children experience in school. Their work highlights the value of a robust attachment experience in the early years and the importance of an experience of containment, by supportive and reflective adults, of frightening and overwhelming feelings. A perfect start in life is hard to come by, but for many children their emotional environment will be good enough. Also, if the closest significant adults in a child's life fall short, a good experience of significant and reliable adults in a wider network can foster resilience in the face of difficulty. Success in school, a facilitating relationship with a teacher, or teachers, and good peer relationships can support the growth of resilience, where things have been unhelpful in the early years (Bion, 1962a; Bowlby , 1988b; Klein, 1931; Winnicott, 1965/1990).

The impact on teachers

Sadly, many children arrive at school with behaviour patterns, developed as a survival strategy, which antagonize or interfere with social and educational relationships. These habits prevent children from achieving success in school. They do not get the help they need to address their thinking difficulties. They resist educational "food" and they may try to take charge or alternatively to disappear in classroom situations. Their behaviour can promote unhelpful reactions in those trying to help. There is little space for teachers to stand back from the experience and recognize that this is the child's stuff and does not have to be taken personally or cause retaliation (Dyke, 1987). Such children often act as irritants or get forgotten. They do not always reach the level of concern which would trigger a request for outside intervention or, if such a move is suggested by the school, parents or carers may reject offers of help.

Group educational psychotherapy in school

In setting up a project of this kind I invite members of the school staff to think about these troubled and troubling children. I discuss concerns and offer to work with a group of six children, using Educational Psychotherapy techniques. In the initial discussions with the staff there is time for some thinking about quiet as well as noisy children, and girls as well as boys. A member of staff is also invited to join me in facilitating a selected group of six children. There are two reasons for this. The first is that children can benefit from an experience of being "thought about" by two adults acting as a co-operative couple. The second is that, as a co-worker to the Educational Psychotherapist, sharing in the facilitation of the group "thinking space", the staff member has a chance to observe how children communicate emotional pain and confusion through words, behaviour, and drawings. Through this involvement the co-workers can explore useful ways of responding to the challenge of hard-to-reach children.

I find it important to offer a presentation to the staff group about the project. There is a danger that a visiting professional will be seen either in an idealized way as one who can solve problems, or in a suspicious way as someone who thinks they know it all. Involving the school staff from the start can bridge a gap, support self-esteem, and encourage more "reflective" responses to challenging children.

Selection of children

Selecting six silent, inhibited, and depressed children would be unhelpful to them and those running the group, as would putting six noisy, competitive, and angry ones together in a group. There needs to be a balance of difficulty, allowing everyone a chance to feel helpful in the way they interact with others. It is noticeable how a child with more energy and noise can draw out a more withdrawn and inhibited one. A rather quieter child can have a calming influence on a more impulsive or aggressive one. A group with children from different classes and year groups allows more space for children to explore different patterns of behaviour. Children from the same class are likely to show more competitive behaviour with each other. In a mixed group older children may be drawn to more thoughtful and empathic behaviour by the presence of younger children.

Parental involvement in the project

Children need to know that parents/carers have been informed and have given permission. Parents/carers are offered a chance to meet with my co-worker and myself before the group sessions begin. Individual appointments give a chance for a discussion of shared or different concerns. Parents/carers can also share any questions or anxieties they may have about the group project.

Problems with group work

Educational Psychotherapy practice demonstrates how children communicate distress through imaginative tasks and can be helped by being given a chance to explore difficult feelings in the context of a reliable relationship, but the thought of working therapeutically with groups rather than individuals can engender anxiety in the school staff. The idea of "therapy" stirs fears of being overwhelmed by knowledge of emotional pain and a fear that "cans of worms" will be opened. However, my experience is that groups of children who work in the presence of two reflective adults, using educational tasks with therapeutic potential, grow in resilience together and resolve some of their problems (Morton, 2000a). The group is different from the classroom, but is within the school setting. The whole experience needs to make sense to the children, while also offering a

new and safe space for thinking about painful or anxious preoccupations. As part of the preparation for the intervention, it is important to have a careful discussion with the school staff about
boundaries.

The group

The therapeutic story group takes place for an hour a week for
twelve weeks. The Educational Psychotherapist and co-worker
introduce the children to each other. There is a regular pattern for
each group. After a simple introductory routine, a collaborative,
turn-taking game is introduced. Then each week the group is helped
to construct a collaborative narrative in which the metaphor of a
journey, usually on a boat, is developed using everyone's ideas,
which are scribed by the adults. At the start of the first group session, the children are helped to select a colour pen as a "marker" for
their ideas. Children's special colours are used in the game and then
in the story. The use of colour indicates that everyone's ideas are
heard and thought about. The collaborative narrative, developed
over a period of about twelve weeks, encourages an experience of
acceptance and belonging.

Understanding and managing behaviour

The message should be that the primary task is about thinking
rather than getting right answers. It is an attempt to develop a reflective (rather than reactive or frozen) capacity in impulsive, controlling, withdrawn or inhibited children selected for the group. The
children's ideas are observed with interest and the two adults will
also notice their behaviour in the group in ways that will be experienced as being benevolently thought about rather than being criticized. To have no rules would leave everyone feeling unsafe, but an
excessively rule-bound setting could block new thinking. Children
need to know from the start that the adults will keep things safe, but
additional rules may evolve from problematic situations as they
arise and the children will be helped by a discussion about what
rules might be usefully set. Children are encouraged to observe and

comment on their peers' patterns of behaviour in kind ways through circular questioning. "Thinking about" can be a more effective way of changing behaviour than just controlling it. In this way an experiential learning opportunity can be provided for the "school adult", who can also explore the powerful effect of using metaphor and school activities to discuss real issues with children and explore emotional pain without opening an overwhelming "can of worms".

The adults' thinking time

Children can evoke different feelings in different adults, partly as a result of specific differences in their life experiences. After each group, time is set aside for the two co-workers to reflect on their experience of the children during the session, to share observations, and to explore different views. Repetitions of behaviour patterns and themes and images in the work are noted and plans for the following session are made on the basis of these discussions.

What happens each week in the group

In the welcoming routine, any absences are acknowledged. Children may express anxieties about who is missing, which may be a way of talking about their own fears. In the turn-taking game it is made clear that the adults will ensure fair play, while they notice and respond to withdrawn or overactive behaviour. A typical game uses Donald Winnicott's idea of "Squiggles" (illustrated by case material in his book "Therapeutic Consultations in Child Psychiatry": Winnicott, 1971b). Each person has a turn to draw a "squiggle" (without looking) using their personal colour. The next person tries to create a picture from this "squiggle". There is no wrong answer. Shy, anxious children can "pass" if they do not have an idea. If children have too many ideas—telling everyone else what to draw for instance—a discussion with the rest of the group takes place, to explore whether the child wants to be too helpful, thus reframing behaviour in a way that the child can hear. Behaviour is thought about rather than just reacted to, but it is made clear that the adults will ensure fairness. Imaginative ideas are acceptable and there is room for a whole range of different ideas.

An example of a group

Rachel, Jimmy, Larry, Mary, Malcolm, and Sammy were selected for a group because of the following problems in school and in their family lives. Rachel was irritatingly demanding, needing constant reassurance, and was clingy, holding hands with the playground supervisor instead of playing. She seemed to reflect her father's anxious over-protection of her, against a background of family loss and fears for her safety. Larry, whose family had arrived from Eastern Europe, was nervously silent in class—well–behaved, but reluctant to participate. He witnessed domestic violence by his father, which his mother was unwilling to expose on account of death threats. Jimmy, on the other hand, was a constant irritation to peers and teachers, hit other children, and name-called, but followed this with "only joking". Disruptive to teachers and peers, he lived with his father, but was no longer allowed contact with his mother on account of her emotional abuse. Mary was very silent and withdrawn, but came from a rather noisy and chaotic home where she needed to be vigilant for upheavals. Malcolm was worrying both his teacher and his mother by his anxious presentation. The mother had let the school know that she and her son had spent a year in fear of a stalker who appeared everywhere they went and had attacked their house at night. Malcolm seemed preoccupied and unable to participate in class activities. Sammy had been unsettled for some time, but was showing more challenging and disruptive behaviour since his mother and her partner, both substance abusers, had been fighting in the street. Sammy was now with foster carers, but plans for his future were not clear.

The collaborative narrative

In the first session of this group, after the introduction and the game of colours, I drew a large outline of a boat and placed this in the centre of the table, saying, "We are going to make a story about a boat journey. All of us need to draw ourselves and think what things we want to bring on the boat." As the children, the teacher, and I started on this task with pens, scissors, and glue, she and I listened for comments and conversations. I wrote down ideas, as I heard them. These included: "We might need emergency supplies/food/ pans", "If people are Christian they should take a Bible and if there is trouble they can read it" (others suggested Muslims taking the Koran), "We need pens and pencils to draw what we see", and "We should take respect with us—you can't ignore it". "Maybe I might bring a telescope." "I will bring my mobile phone to stay in touch." "I'm bringing danger-flares and ropes as we may crash into an iceberg." The teacher and I made suggestions too, such as a photo album for everyone who wanted to bring a photo of someone at home, a first aid box, and a large old Story Book.

A first session usually ends with everyone having a self-portrait and objects stuck onto the boat. Children may draw themselves as huge or tiny, disguised in some way (e.g., as a pirate, a poisonous creature, or a robot who knows everything) or as a very recognizable self-portrait. One boy drew himself seated on a dragon, which flew along behind the boat. The story thus begins as, metaphorically, everyone gets on board with their stuff and the children all realize, through using their individual colours, that their ideas have been accepted in the story.

The story chapters

The story we make has a beginning, some metaphoric travelling, and an ending in which the journey is completed. Chapter headings for the story might look like this:

- We are going on a boat in our story. What shall we take with us?
- What is that over there under the water?
  (Children wonder out loud what it might be and their ideas are written into the story in their personal colours. Conversations between children are included when they discuss different possibilities. In this and each following chapter the children have opportunities to express their ideas and have them accepted; they see their words being recorded in the collaborative story, but can also draw their own particular versions of the story to put in a personal folder.)
- The sky's getting dark and the boat is moving about a lot.
- What is in that floating box?

- There is something that looks like a bottle floating over there. Has it got a message written inside it?
- I can see land, can you?
- Should we go and explore or not?
- I can see a book in the sand. It says "Amazing Book of Stories". I wonder what stories we think could be in the book.
- I can hear a noise coming from that cave in the rocks. Is it a creature? What does it look like and what is it saying?
- It is time to go home—what will we remember?

Metaphor and communication

Each chapter presents opportunities to think about uncertainty, danger, and challenge, and to communicate fears and expectations about the outside world and relationships. The "box in the water", for instance, is one of the many receptacles we offer for children's communications about feared or longed-for objects, events, and experiences. There might be a baby needing food, or a dead person. There might be treasure, or a map, or deadly weapons. The box might be a trap, or a trick to lure us into danger. It could be a mirage instead of land ahead. "The sky's getting dark" prompts thoughts such as— Will we survive a storm? Will the adults stop the boat from breaking up? What or who is on the island? Wonderful food? A place of starvation, abandonment, and unreliable adults? Some children's responses highlight their vigilance about potential disasters. Others exhibit unsuspected problem-solving skills. They all experience their ideas of being heard and remembered and incorporated into something bigger than themselves or their individual ideas.

The use of a metaphor constructs a boundaried new thinking space, which relieves the child of the need to constantly react, or communicate awful thoughts, through their behaviour towards others. Children take part in the story-making in different ways. At first, some want to hog both the ideas and the time. Others cannot find the courage to join in. Some copy another child's ideas. In the first few sessions the therapist demonstrates that all ideas can be listened to, that things will be written in each person's colour to show that they have been heard and that everything will be kept safe in the group box for the next time.

The therapeutic journey

As each week goes by, the teacher and I keep the endless possibilities in the story alive by maintaining the language of hypotheses. This is the tricky bit. We suggest that we can guess what might be under the sea, in a box floating past, or in a cave on a strange island, but we may never know the answer. We challenge the children to stay with uncertainty, but everyone's guesses are taken seriously. We try to avoid the tyranny of the majority or the bullying of the loudest voice and we encourage memory, empathy, and tolerance of difference. The two adults, as captains of the ship, keep things safe from utter disaster, while acknowledging fears that adults may not always keep you safe. My co-worker and I thought together about Sammy's view that he, not us, should be in charge. He thought he was better equipped to take care of things than the adults in the group. This seemed understandable given his experience of carers who fought and, at the time, were providing nothing reliable in his life. We commented on this wish to mutiny, which seemed an expression of an understandable lack of faith in adults, while keeping in our role as benevolent authority figures.

After working on each collaborative chapter, the children are given the chance to draw their individual ideas. These can be shown to the rest of the group at the end of the session if they wish, or just placed in individual folders. A wish not to show to others is noticed, but allowed. Mary wanted to keep her pictures to herself. It has been useful in such moments to ask others in the group if they have ideas about why a child might not want to show their work. Children can find it very reassuring to feel thought about by peers in this way and it can often lead to a more open presentation and a lessening of anxiety. Mary became more open as the weeks went by, enjoying the positive comments of the others when this happened.

Anxieties are expressed indirectly through the story, but may lead to an acknowledgement of more global worries. In a group, in November 2001, I wrote my chapter prompt: "And now the sky is looking a bit dark. I wonder why?" Usually this leads to a discussion of an approaching storm and children show fears and also some problem-solving. Some indicate their pessimistic view of the world where adults cannot keep things safe and help never arrives. Others imagine a more omnipotent outcome where single-handedly they save us all. Two months after September 11, 2001, a young boy suggested that the darkness came from a cloud coming from a tall building. He drew a plane flying towards the building. The children discussed this and wondered if he was talking about the twin towers and he agreed "yes—New York—that is what I meant". He seemed relieved to know that his fears were shared. It was a vivid reminder to us that children are often rather overwhelmed by "News" of fearful events. Some lack help from family members, who are unable to tune into these anxieties. These fears can then lurk beneath the surface preventing full attention to school tasks and learning.

The adults' example of "taking children seriously" is taken up by the children as the group progresses. Overall, the story challenges the children to listen and respond to each other. A sign of therapeutic change can be that children's ideas begin to interweave. This may show in their inclusion of everybody in their drawings (in appropriate individual colours); or in remembering each other's ideas. In the previously mentioned example group, Rachel acknowledged one of Jimmy's ideas about some magic potion and suggested it might help with Larry's idea about getting coconuts from a very tall tree. On one occasion Mary, the most withdrawn and unengaged child in the group, had chosen in a whisper to bring a telescope on board. Sammy suggested using Mary's telescope to see what was on the horizon. Mary smiled shyly for the first time at this example of her idea being "taken in" and remembered by another child. The telescope became a group object, featured in several story chapters and was mentioned by everyone, but Mary's ownership was always acknowledged by the children. In the same way the group adopted Jimmy's laptop and thus challenged his convictions about their lack of appreciation of his ideas. This had an impact on his habitual provocative approach to his peers, both in the group and in his class.

As the boat undergoes its voyage, children show their preoccupations in various ways. For example, strange creatures may be seen along the way, which are given characteristics of internalized negative or positive figures. Malcolm kept seeing a "seaweed monster" that followed our boat through the storm and pursued Malcolm onto the uninhabited island. He was cornered by the dangerous creature, but the whole of the group decided to help him in his hour of need. They killed the creature in the story, and in their own pictures, and the boy was made safe. The seaweed monster, who would not go away and kept appearing as a threatening presence, suggested to me the aggressive stalker who in real life had followed Malcolm and his mother for a year and attempted to break into their house. The teacher and I thought about this connection, but we decided not to make a direct link in the group. Malcolm's confidence increased as the story progressed and he was able to describe his preoccupations "in the metaphor" to others. His classroom behaviour changed markedly and we felt that his use of the metaphoric space for thinking about the fearful events had freed him to be able to think again in class.

In the same way, Larry showed in one session that his experience of domestic violence was always near the surface. We started that session by suggesting that all the children had had a dream after a storm. Larry drew his dream picture rapidly. He asked the teacher to write "I had a bad dream that the monsters were fighting and the monster woman was saying 'stop it, stop it'. The babies were crying." His individual drawing seemed a vivid depiction, in a metaphor, of what was most in his mind. Without making any direct reference to Larry's family life my co-worker and I talked about how frightened small children would be if adults were fighting. We wanted to acknowledge Larry's communication without breaking the family rule about not speaking of the violence. (As a result of the group project in school, Larry's mother was able to seek help for a safer life for herself and her children, but there is no space here to give details.)

A chapter prompt about an island usually stirs a lot of different ideas. (Will it be full of fun like a playground? Maybe it is full of pirates who like to kidnap or kill children. Maybe there could be treasure.) Rachel, reflecting her father's anxieties, referred to land that would not stay still, not being able to trust what you see, and girls being in danger with no hope of rescue. She drew a girl on an island being covered with lava from a volcano. Jimmy drew a crowd of children (with blank faces) on the island who were all crying out for their mother. Sammy wondered if the island was a mirage, not to be trusted.

Once on the island, children are asked to imagine what might be in a cave. At this stage of the group children seem to get more easily in touch with contradictory or unacceptable aspects of self. Larry thought a cave on the island contained a monster. After drawing the monster he labelled it with his own name saying quietly "I am a monster. I lose my temper and throw things". Rachel's drawing echoed earlier fearful pictures of a girl in danger. Throughout the project, her repeated image of lightning suggested a constant threat of disaster. Even within the cave, the lightning flashed down at the girl in the picture. Repetitions of an image such as this, like Malcolm's ongoing Seaweed Monster, can be thought of as a vivid communication about the ongoing and not-yet-understood worries in the child.

Returning home—bringing the group to a good end

Ending the group is managed with the help of the metaphoric journey. Ambivalence about leaving the story island to return home often stirs anxieties, which need to be heard. Rachel was sure we could not return "because we had lost the map". She thought that we needed to stay on the island. Jimmy suggested he had a map on his mobile phone, which we could use, but Rachel replied that it had fallen in the sea and been eaten by a shark. It was clear that Rachel was wishing we had more time. Larry had a wish for sudden rescue by helicopter. The children were asked to draw some things they would remember about the journey to send on a postcard home— "to let people at home know we will be back soon". It was important to acknowledge the wish to stay as well as to reinforce the reality of the ending.

The children were told that they would have one more meeting at a later date in which they could share and read the final copy of the story to an invited senior member of staff. This would be typed in their colours and include examples of their pictures. They would also get a copy to take home. This is our usual practice when ending a group.

The group as container

Children who have experienced extremes of fear, helplessness, secrecy, loss, and other things that are hard to think about, without help from a "holding" (Winnicott, 1965/1990) and "containing"

(Bion, 1962b) carer, understandably find it hard to manage in school. Tasks and relationships in class and playground prove a huge challenge. Among other factors, resilience seems to be promoted by an experience of school competence, by good peer relationships, and by being in the presence of adults who are able to stay with and bear emotional pain and confusion so that the unthinkable can be thought about. Children may have to keep family rules of silence about danger, as in Larry's case; or like Jimmy lack help or permission to think about the loss of a mother who was both longed for and emotionally abusive; or like Rachel be confused by overprotection from imagined dangers and secrecy about significant family history. Mary had learned that it was better to be invisible, and Sammy that adults are less reliable than oneself. Working with a collaborative narrative, the children were offered the opportunity to express, in a metaphor, their emotional obstacles to thinking. They experienced their ideas being received and respected by others. This process can, belatedly, give children something of the kind of experience of empathic relationships that securely attached children have experienced in their early development and which encourage the development of thinking and a capacity for reflection (Hobson, 2007). They experience being benevolently thought about by other minds and observe different strategies of behaviour. They become curious about other ways of doing things, and experience being helpful. Through engaging in imaginative tasks their skills are improved and they gain confidence in putting things on paper. The resulting group book of the journey gives affirmation of their contributions as it is typed in their colours and contains their pictures. The book is also concrete evidence of how adults can bear and hold onto their fears and fantasies.

What we hope for and what can happen

A short intervention such as this does not produce magical cures, but it does help schools to broaden their understanding of how children communicate their difficult thoughts and emotions. It demonstrates to the school staff how school activities can provide, at one remove, a space for thinking together. When parents are invited to meet with the teacher and therapist, this can lead to a shift in home–school relations. Children benefit from being thought about by two reflective adults—a clear resilience builder. This experience has often been lacking in the family lives of the problematic children we work with. Children develop reflectivity themselves and appreciate seeing it in their peers. A more hopeful view may develop and, having less need to hide behind disruptive or silent behaviour, the children can begin to experience success both socially and academically.

How a
one page profile
(+ its PCP process)
can
be therapeutic

CHAPTER TEN

What can educational psychotherapy teach teachers?

Marie Delaney

P rior to training as an Educational Psychotherapist, I worked for many years in various settings as a teacher for pupils with social, emotional, and behaviour disorders (SEBDs) and those considered "at risk" of exclusion from school. My work has involved training staff in primary and secondary schools in behaviour management techniques for these challenging pupils. Throughout my training as an Educational Psychotherapist I was interested in how ideas from Educational Psychotherapy could benefit mainstream teachers. There were times when I struggled with the two roles of teacher and therapist, wondering if they were in fact mutually exclusive. However, as my training progressed, I became convinced that it was possible to use learning from Educational Psychotherapy to support and develop the skills of teachers in mainstream schools. Educational Psychotherapy offered me a new framework for thinking about behaviour—both of pupils and the adults they come into contact with. It seemed possible to combine therapy and teaching in a way that would be beneficial for pupils and staff. In this chapter I hope to describe some of the ideas I have found useful and how I have tried to convey these ideas, in training workshops, to teachers who may be wary of therapy.

Why is therapy threatening?

I began by wondering why therapy is such a threatening word for many staff in schools. I have often heard "Well, I am not a therapist" or "He/she needs specialist therapy" in response to some of my suggestions for dealing with a particular pupil. When running an on-site unit for pupils at risk of exclusion, I was often surprised at how reluctant some teachers seemed to be to try out certain strategies with pupils with challenging behaviour. Even the seemingly more enlightened staff would say the ideas were interesting, but not relevant to a class of 30 pupils. I began to wonder why thinking about behaviour in a different way seemed so difficult at times in schools. Perhaps it is the lack of shared knowledge about each others' professions that can lead to unhelpful assumptions.

When working with teaching staff, I have often begun by asking them to make a list of the differences between therapy and teaching. They have usually produced a long list very quickly. Groups of school staff—both teaching and non-teaching—have come up with remarkably similar lists.

They would usually include:

Teaching	Therapy
Teacher-centred	Client-centred
Imposed curriculum	Topic comes from client
Public	Private
Group	One-to-one
Subject-focused	Emotions can be the focus
Talking	Listening
Accountable to others	Accountable to the client
Short on time	Have time to think
Not paid for by client	Paid for by client
Poor behaviour unhelpful	Poor behaviour can be helpful
Teacher knows	Client knows
Teacher has power	Client has power

It quickly becomes apparent that many of the items on the therapy side of these lists could, and perhaps should, be applied to education. Most teachers and their managers would want their classes to be child-centred with time for thinking. Most would like to think they listen to their pupils and that they can take account of the emotional aspects of learning.

I sometimes then look, with the teachers, at what they think makes a good learner. I encourage them to think about the emotional aspects and we compile a list of attributes of "a good learner", which tends to include:

- feels safe, willing to take risks
- good self-esteem
- can seek help when needed without expecting criticism or ridicule
- able to concentrate, be in the "flow"
- able to manage frustration, anxiety, disappointment
- capacity to bear not knowing
- optimistic and positive attitude to a problem
- can wait for attention

Having elicited such opinions, I believe it is important to look at some of the comments in the columns and challenge the underlying preconceptions. We look at the issue of time and how teachers view therapeutic approaches as taking up too much time. We discuss how we make time for things we think are important and consider questions such as: How long does it take to reflect on the emotion or feeling being projected onto you by a young person and is this any longer than it takes to end up in a damaging confrontation? How long does it take to remember what football team a pupil supports and show them they are being, as Bion would say, "held in mind"?

Furthermore, when I remind the staff that the inherent Latin meaning of "educare" means to draw or lead out, it leads to an interesting discussion about the real reasons the expectations listed on the right hand, or "therapy", side of the page are so difficult to attain in the classroom.

Why is it difficult to make teaching like therapy?

One of the main inhibiting factors I feel lies in the relationships that pupils with SEBDs can invoke. Pupils with challenging behaviour stir up strong emotions in staff—both at a conscious and unconscious level. Sue Panter writes: "It must be recognized that the area of pupil behaviour is highly emotive. It challenges teachers' sense of their own professional competence and both teachers' and parents' self-esteem; emotions often get in the way of constructive planning" (Gray & Panter, 2000).

I would suggest, therefore, that an understanding of psychodynamic concepts, including unconscious mental processes, can help staff understand and deal with their feelings and behaviour, in order to deal better with those of their pupils.

When starting a training day, I have often begun with a drawing done by a pupil in a secondary school where I was working. In one school I was supervising the Learning Mentors and suggested they ask this boy to draw a self-portrait. John was a year 7 pupil, who was constantly running out of class, could not settle, and was rude to teachers who tried to talk to him about it. When frustrated, he would bang his head against the wall. I show this drawing to a staff group, without giving them the background information, and ask them to tell me their initial feelings and thoughts. It is important that they do not take too long as I want their "gut" reaction. Generally, there is a feeling of fear—either that the picture makes them fearful or they think the boy is fearful. Some people also comment on the mouth and lack of ears—as if the boy is screaming and no-one is listening. I explain to the group that this picture can tell us a lot about this pupil's world and that by listening to our own feelings we can begin to find a way into a dialogue with the pupil. If we can think of ourselves as observing rather than judging, we can find cues to enable us to discuss matters with the pupil. I use this as a good example of how pupils can communicate a great deal non-verbally and project their feelings into us. If we are feeling frightened, maybe it is because the pupil is overwhelmingly frightened. A key way of working with this type of pupil is to show that we can cope with this overwhelming feeling; that we can "contain" feelings projected into us and, in Bion's terms, give them back in a more digestible form. The problem is that pupils with SEBDs often stir up literally "unbearable" feelings in us and the natural reaction might well be to push them away or deny them—hence, the comments such as "I'm not a therapist". Interestingly, in any staff group, there is usually one member who insists that the drawing could be based on something from the TV or fantasy world and that "we shouldn't read too much into it." I feel at this point they may need reassurance that this might be the case, taken out of context, but that in this context it did actually give us a way of talking to the young person about his feelings. I believe that the teacher who wanted the drawing to be just a cartoon character, found the feelings too unbearable to think about. I would also wonder with this teacher why a child would choose to represent himself as a scary monster.

It becomes apparent that it is not necessarily therapeutic *techniques* that are difficult to pass on to teachers, but rather a way of thinking. What stops them from embracing this way of thinking?

In fairness to the staff in schools, I believe that not much attention is paid to the teachers' own emotions and feelings. There is an emphasis now on introducing Emotional Literacy and Social, Emotional, and Affective Learning into UK schools, but how much time is given to the teachers to explore their feelings? In my experience young people come into school and behave pretty much the same each day: what differs is the reaction of the adults and this is usually linked to their own state of mind and emotions. I include an exercise called "Mapping of States" in my teacher training. I ask the participants to write down all the emotional states they have been through on the previous day, from the time they got up to the time they went to bed. This usually shows an incredible roller-coaster of emotions, with some people going from "elation" to "depression" in a couple of hours! The next stage is to think about which states are productive for learning and which are not. We can then look at how to maintain the productive states and get out of the unproductive states. When doing this activity with a group of teachers in Romford, Essex, I was amazed by how animated and involved everyone became. One teacher became very angry and said her main state in the day was of anger and tiredness and she did not see why she was not allowed to be angry if young people were continually being challenging and abusive. We discussed that it is acceptable to feel angry and considered the difference between acknowledging the feeling and acting on it. This made me realize that we do this work in schools with young people, but rarely with the staff. My training as an Educational Psychotherapist allowed me to think about the need for adults to act, in Bion's terms, as "containers", and what is needed for the "container" to be strong. Supervision and personal therapy are important require-ments of training for any psychodynamic therapy but not for teaching. Teachers, at times, seem to experience themselves as being blamed for all society's ailments and have to cope with a maelstrom of very strong, often unbearable, emotions. We have to wonder where they are meant to off-load and process their own reactions and thoughts.

How can education learn from therapy?

When it becomes clear that the teachers are troubled by the strong emotions aroused in them in their work it can be useful to look at a few psychodynamic concepts, which I have learnt from my Educational Psychotherapy training and found useful as a teacher. Bearing in mind the potential mistrust of psychotherapy, I like to de-mystify it so that teachers feel it is something accessible and something they can learn from. I start, therefore, by asking them to think about the meaning of certain words from the point of view of common sense and previous knowledge. Following on from our discussions in the tasks outlined above, and once the teachers have become aware of the importance of understand-ing and reflecting on their own emotions and their part in the pupil–teacher relationship, I can introduce the idea of defence mechanisms. These are things we do unconsciously to protect ourselves from "unbearable" feelings. The defences I choose to name are:

- Projection
- Transference
- Displacement

(See discussion on transference and defence mechanisms in Chapter Two.)

In any staff group, there is usually a good attempt to understand the meaning of these words in a teaching context and we look at the following explanations to clarify the concepts.

Summary for teachers

Psychological defence mechanisms

Psychological Defence Mechanisms are ways in which people protect themselves from fear or anxiety and avoid conscious awareness of emotional conflict. The following are examples of the common defence mechanisms and ways in which teachers can become aware of how these defences operate in a school situation.

Projection

Unbearable, painful, or disturbing feelings are externalized by pushing them out and attributing them to others.

Awareness of projection and an appropriate response

The way you are feeling when with a child may give you an indication of what *they* are feeling. Our task is to recognize which feelings are our own and which have been projected into us. Unbearable feelings need to be contained, named, and given back in a "digested" and acceptable form. If they are not received and contained by the adult, the child may feel there is no acceptance or understanding of these feelings. Instead of the terrible feelings being made tolerable, the child can re-introject what Bion calls a "nameless dread" (Bion, 1962b).

Displacement

An emotion is displaced from one person or situation to another. For example, a separation anxiety due to a depressed or ill parent can lead to a school phobia. A child who has experienced domestic violence at home may, on one level, feel angry towards the parent for allowing this to happen, but will feel guilty about expressing this anger. The anger may then be turned towards a teacher in school— sometimes the teacher that has tried to help them the most.

Awareness of displacement and an appropriate response

Look for an underlying cause in another situation. For example, a bully may use power at school because of feeling powerless at home. The need for help with the home situation would then be indicated.

Transference

Transference is a mechanism where feelings and attitudes experienced in a relationship with a main carer in the past are "transferred" and re-experienced in a later relationship, for example, with a teacher.

Awareness of transference and an appropriate response

A child's seemingly inexplicable reaction to a member of staff may be triggered by their being reminded of someone else by that person. Our own reaction to a child may relate to our own experience of another relationship.

Understanding that a child's attitude, for example, a hostile provocative attitude towards a particular teacher, may be related to the child's hostile relationship with a parent, can help the teacher to take the child's hostility less personally. This makes it easier to contain the feelings provoked by the child's hostility.

Similarly, realizing that a child reminds you of someone you dislike can also help you to disentangle the feelings about that other person from your reaction to that child.

Containment

Containment, a concept already used in describing the previous examples, is a theoretical concept that is very useful to teachers.

As already mentioned, I find it helpful to explain some of Bion's theory of containment to teachers. This can come as a relief when the teacher realizes that they do not always need immediate solutions and strategies to deal with a display of emotion. If they can learn to bear the feeling, help the pupil to name it, and give it back in a more "digestible" form, they could be allowing a pupil to have the experience of being understood and held in mind. Being thought about allows us to develop the capacity to think (Bion, 1962b). Winnicott states that

> Naming makes shared and therefore socially acceptable, what was previously private fantasy, gives greater self-awareness and therefore control, allows fantasy to be checked with reality, increases capacity to remember and reduces guilt. It is not, therefore, a failure to interpret. [Hopkins, 2002, p. 93]

Attachment theory (see Chapter One)

I have found it useful to present some of the main ideas from Bowlby's attachment theory, and Ainsworth's later work, to staff groups. In particular, I believe it allows them to think differently about the behaviour of children when other strategies have often failed. I do not present it as the answer to all problems, but encourage staff to see it as another tool, another way of thinking which may shed light on or "reframe" a problem. I encourage staff to think about each category and reflect on strategies for themselves. I believe this allows them to make their own links between theory and practice, which is vital if teachers are to learn to apply this new way of thinking to their work and experience the benefit in terms of their pupils' responses to their increased therapeutic understanding. I present them with the following short descriptions and ask them to think about possible teaching strategies based on the information.

Summary for teachers

Attachment theory

John Bowlby developed Attachment Theory, based on research evidence (see Chapter One). He concluded that infants are genetically pre-programmed to develop attachment behaviour towards their primary caregiver—usually the mother. Bowlby's work was developed further, arising from research undertaken by Mary Ainsworth, who discovered three distinct patterns of attachment behaviour in young children: securely attached, insecure/ambivalent-resistant, insecure/avoidant. A fourth pattern of insecure/disorganized/disorientated attachment behaviour was later identified by Mary Main.

Secure attachment behaviour pattern

Securely attached children develop basic trust and confidence that others will be helpful when asked. They generally cope better in schools than insecurely attached children, as they have learnt to play independently, take risks, ask for help, can wait for attention, and relate positively to peers and teachers.

Insecure attachment

Insecure: anxious–ambivalent/resistant behaviour pattern

These children cannot predict their mother's response and so are reluctant to leave her side. In school they are often very anxious; overly dependent on the teacher; unable to take independent action; need constant reassurance; find it hard to focus on a task in case they lose the attention of the teacher; tend to use oral language very skilfully, but underachieve in relation to written verbal skills.

Awareness of insecure anxious–ambivalent/resistant behaviour pattern and an appropriate response in class

Awareness of a child's anxious–ambivalent/resistant behaviour pattern can enable a teacher to make clear to the child that he/she is kept in mind and engage him/her in school work by, for example, setting small timed tasks, making sure the child knows the teacher will be back to check in a certain number of minutes, and not colluding with the "clingy" behaviour.

Insecure avoidant attachment behaviour pattern

These children develop patterns of avoidant behaviour as they expect rebuff and rejection. In class they often show apparent indifference to anxiety in a new situation; they deny the need for support and help from the teacher and do not like the teacher to stand in close proximity, they need to be autonomous and involved in the task, they show limited use of communication and creative opportunities.

Awareness of insecure avoidant attachment and an appropriate response

On discussing the problems of Insecure Avoidant children with groups of teachers, the teachers have come up with their own constructive ideas for working effectively with these children, such as:

- relating to the pupil through the task
- allowing them space to work
- giving non-public and/or written praise
- not colluding by avoiding contact with the child, but not being overly intrusive in a desire to show you care

Insecure/disorganised/disorientated attachment

These children often develop controlling behaviour towards their parents and other adults, sometimes in a punitive way. They have very impoverished relationships. In class they may be very agitated and over-reactive or "switch off". Parents may be unlikely to engage with support services.

Awareness of insecure/disorganised attachment and an appropriate response

Here it is essential for professionals to work together and support each other.

Teachers who have experience of working with such children emphasize the need for clear structures and the signalling of any changes, which are seen as catastrophic by this type of pupil.

I suggest that teachers think of a pupil for each type and reflect on this way of viewing their behaviour. This kind of reflective thinking about theoretical concepts can be a productive way for a teacher to come up with strategies for understanding and dealing with challenging behaviour.

Winnicott's theories about play

I have also found it helpful to talk a little about Donald Winnicott's theories about play (Winnicott, 1971a). I usually elicit from staff the stages of play, which show that being able to play by someone else's rules is the final and most developed stage of play. Most children who get into trouble at school are not at this stage of play developmentally and, quite literally, cannot play by the rules of the teacher and school. This is usually a very different way of thinking about behaviour for most staff and can lead to fruitful discussions about the need to develop play at all ages.

What leads schools to "sabotage" therapy?

I am also interested in the reasons therapy can be sabotaged by schools. Colleagues who have undertaken to see children for regular therapy sessions in a school often report rooms not being made available, children who cannot be found, and staff who insist a pupil cannot attend this "reward" as they have been badly behaved. I think it is helpful to understand this as an example of envy and spoiling. Melanie Klein defines envy as "the angry feeling that another person possesses and enjoys something desirable, the envious impulse being to take away or spoil it" (Klein, 1963). In fact, I believe, most staff would love some individual thinking and talking time for themselves and they see the naughtiest children in the school getting it. On an unconscious level, sibling rivalry and spoiling can kick in. When I worked as a co-ordinator for Learning Mentors in a London Borough, I attempted to suggest that Learning Mentors should have supervision for their work, as they were dealing with very complex and emotionally draining cases. This provoked an angry response from some of the headteachers who said they dealt with this kind of thing every day and no-one offered them supervision. One headteacher retorted angrily "I know what you are going to say, Marie, you are going to say we should all have it". I replied that I did indeed think that all headteachers could benefit from supervision, but someone not having something was not a reason not to give it to the Learning Mentors. Afterwards, I reflected on this rather childish exchange, and came to the conclusion that actually therapy is dangerous for these heads as it makes them realize their own difficulties and desire for supervision. By acknowledging the need, it is as if we are pointing out that the Emperor is not wearing any clothes.

Being able to reflect on my interactions with teaching staff in a psychodynamic framework, has helped me to think more kindly of colleagues when it seems that they want to dismiss my work or ideas. It has given me another way of thinking about their reactions and, potentially, of more strategies for communicating with them.

What can Educational Psychotherapists bring to schools?

I believe that Educational Psychotherapists have an important role to play in developing "thinking" schools, which allow the staff space to reflect. By bringing in a different way of thinking, they can help de-stress the staff and empower them to deal more effectively with challenging behaviour. For example, I am employed as an Emotional Literacy consultant in a secondary school in Romford. The headteacher is a very resourceful person, who is excellent in crises—except when a pupil sets off the fire alarm. Recently, in a discussion in the corridor, a member of staff suggested to the head that it was interesting to note who usually set the alarm off—normally pupils from a low-ability class with very little self-esteem. She likened it to a "cry for help". The head-teacher took this on board as a very different way of thinking about a disruptive behaviour. If we could bring more of this type of re-framing into schools, we would be building their capacity and resilience. Incidentally, initially I thought this young teacher would make an excellent Educational Psychotherapist. Now I believe she should become an excellent, therapeutically thinking, headteacher!

This example shows that educational psychotherapists do not always need to be involved in staff training to make a difference. A conversation in a corridor can help re-frame behaviour and contribute a different way of thinking. Robert Coles quotes Anna Freud as stressing the need for "careful, detailed, open-minded observation of children and theoretical conceptualization" (Coles, 1992). Through their conversations and their own comments, educational psychotherapists can help staff in schools think in this way.

I realize that what I have written is a simplification of complex, in-depth, psychoanalytical theories. I hope this makes these ideas accessible to those working in mainstream education so that we can collaborate to help more pupils by facilitating the development of a reflective, thinking approach, rather than a reactive, non-thinking one.

We need to look at our common goals. As teachers and therapists we are often looking for the underlying meaning, in seemingly inexplicable behaviour, in order to help children make sense of their experience and resolve some of their problems. It is rarely possible to address this by looking only at what is directly observable. For example, a child often cannot explain why he/she has chosen to act in a seemingly destructive or challenging way at school. By trying to understand what is happening in their internal models of the world and how it is affecting us, we can sometimes gain deeper insight into children's problems.

"So what?"—what are the teaching strategies?

In any training with mainstream staff, they will want to get to what I call the "so what?" factor—what can they do differently the next day in their lessons to apply some of the thinking and concepts? I will finish, therefore, by suggesting some ideas for staff to take away and try out.

Summary for teachers

Teaching strategies influenced by therapeutic thinking

- Be clear that emotional health is as important as physical health. Pay attention to your own emotional state and have strategies for getting into a positive state for teaching and learning. Share these strategies with learners, for example, thinking of a beautiful place, listening to a song, going for a walk.
- Listen to the feelings underlying communications with you. Be prepared to name the feelings, particularly the overwhelming emotions. Many of the children we deal with do not have a vocabulary for naming and recognizing feelings, which leads to their feelings being suppressed and then exploding.
- Encourage pupils to develop a vocabulary of feelings. Anger is often a secondary emotion, so help them find a word to describe how they are feeling. "I wonder if you are now feeling really disappointed and let down".
- Use creative activities to help pupils explore feelings in a safe, "contained" way, for example, stories, drawings, modelling, games, videos, soaps.
- Develop activities which allow recognition and acceptance of negative feelings, for example, competitive games such as hangman or battleships.
- Teach children how to express their aggression in a socially acceptable way and to win and lose safely.

- Make sure children know that it is not the *feelings* that are bad. We all have bad feelings; we need to acknowledge them to ourselves before we can decide how to deal with them and whether or how to express them or act on them.
- Make a safe place for children to vent their difficult feelings safely. Make sure pupils know how to access this, for example, a worry box. It is impossible to learn when not motivated, or when feeling too bad. All activities that help pupils manage their emotional states and improve their self-esteem will help to increase their enjoyment in learning and achievement.

Suggestions to headteachers, heads of year, and other senior school staff

Ensure that all the staff know the importance of emotions in learning, discuss it with them, help them to manage their own states. Encourage the setting up of staff support facilitation groups. Admitting to not knowing something or feeling overwhelmed is not a weakness.

- Encourage staff to have a "check in" with feelings at various stages in their lessons
- Provide assertiveness training
- Provide leadership skills training for key pupils, including training on naming feelings
- Do not be afraid to start small. Even your own use of language, and re-framing, can affect change
- Remember that Winnicott talks about "good-enough mothering". There is also "good-enough" teaching. You do not need to be perfect. You need to be prepared to think about the good and the bad
- When talking to upset pupils, allow them to express their negative feelings without jumping immediately to a false reassurance
- Discuss with pupils the difference between having a feeling and acting on it
- Ask open-ended questions to which you are genuinely curious to know the answer

• See delinquent behaviour as telling us something; for example,
  about cheating/lying you could comment "You really can't
  bear to lose"

Perhaps, therefore, the divide between teaching and therapy is
not as great as it sometimes seems.

REFERENCES

Ainsworth, M. D. S., & Wittig, B. A. (1969). Attachment and exploratory behavior of one-year olds in a strange situation. In: W. B. Foss (Ed.), *Determinants of Infant Behaviour* (Vol. 4, pp. 111–136). London: Methuen.

Alvarez, A. (1992). *Live Company*. London: Routledge.

Barrett, M., & Trevitt, J. (1991). *Attachment Behaviour and the Schoolchild*. London: Tavistock/Routledge.

Barrows, K. (1984). A child's difficulties in using his gifts and his imagination. *Journal of Child Psychotherapy*, 10(1): 15–26.

Bettelheim, B. (1976). *The Uses of Enchantment*. London: Penguin Books.

Bettelheim, B. (1992). *Recollections and Reflections*. London: Penguin Books.

Bettelheim, B., & Zelan, K. (1981). *On Learning to Read: The Child's Fascination with Meaning*. London: Thames & Hudson & Penguin Books.

Bick, E. (1968). The experience of the skin in early object relations. *International Journal of Psychoanalysis*, 49: 484–488.

Bion, W. R. (1962a). *Learning from Experience*. London: Heinemann.

Bion, W. R. (1962b). The psycho-analytic study of thinking. II. A theory of thinking. *International Journal of Psychoanalysis*, 43: 306–310.

Bion, W. R. (1967). *Second Thoughts* (pp. 110–119). London: Karnac. Reprinted (1987 & 1990).

Boston, M., & Szur, R.. (1983). *Psychotherapy with Severely Disturbed Children*. London: Routledge & Kegan Paul.

Bowlby, J. (1988a). On knowing what you are not supposed to know and feeling what you are not supposed to feel. In: *A Secure Base: Clinical Applications of Attachment Theory* (pp. 99–118). London: Routledge.

Bowlby, J. (1988b). The role of attachment in personality development. In: *A Secure Base: Clinical Applications of Attachment Theory* (pp. 119–136). London: Routledge.

Byng-Hall, J. (1973). Family myths used as a defence: conjoint family therapy. In: *Developments in Family Therapy: Theories and Applications Since 1948* (Chapter 6, pp. 105–120). London: Routledge & Kegan Paul.

Caspari, I. (1974a). Educational therapy. In: V. Varma, (Ed.), *Psychotherapy Today* (pp. 215–232). London: Constable.

Caspari, I. (1974b). Parents as co-therapists, a family approach to the treatment of reading disability. Tavistock Clinic Doc No EN781.

Caspari, I. (1986). *Learning and Teaching: The Collected Papers of Irene Caspari*. London: Caspari Foundation.

Coles, R. (1992). *The Dream of Psychoanalysis*. Cambridge, Massachusetts: Perseus Publishing.

Cummings, E. M., & Davies, P. (1994). *Children and Marital Conflict*. New York: Guilford Press.

Damasio, A. (1999). *The Feeling of What Happens*. London: Heinemann.

Delaney, M. (2009). *Teaching the Unteachable*. London: Worth Publishing.

Delaney, M. (2010). *"What can I do with the kid who?"* London: Worth Publishing.

Dover, J. (1996). Educational therapy with a latency child. In: M. Barrett & V. Varma (Eds.), *Educational Therapy in Clinic and Classroom* (pp. 16–26). London: Whurr Publishers.

Dover, J. (2002). The child who cannot bear being taught. *Psychodynamic Practice*, 8: 311–325.

Dyke, S. (1987). Psychoanalytic insight in the classroom: asset or liability? *Journal of Educational Therapy*, 1(4): 43–63.

Emanuel, R. (2000). *Anxiety*. Cambridge UK: Icon Books.

Fonagy, P., Steele, M., & Steele, H. (1994). The Emanuel Miller memorial lecture: the theory and practice of resilience. *Journal of Child Psychology and Psychiatry* 35(2): 231–257.

Freud, A. (1937). *The Ego and the Mechanisms of Defence*. London: Hogarth. Reprinted (1986).

Freud, S. (1917). Mourning and melancholia. In: *Standard Edition of the Works of Sigmund Freud* (Vol. XIV, pp. 243–258). London: Hogarth Press.

Geddes, H. (2006a). *Attachment in the Classroom: the Links Between Children's Early Experience, Emotional Well-Being and Performance in School.* London: Worth Publishing.

Geddes, H. (2006b). How can educational therapy help children with attachment issues? *Special Needs Journal, 33*: 101–104.

Geddes, H. (2006c). Troubled children in school – the adopted child. *Adoption Today* October 2006: 20–21.

Goldberg, S. (2000). *Attachment and Development.* London: Arnold.

Gomnaes, I. L. (1988). The use of a fairy tale in educational therapy. *The Journal of Educational Therapy* 2(2): 18–44.

Hanko, G. (1999). *Increasing Competence through Collaborative. Problem Solving: Using insight into social and emotional factors in children's learning.* London: David Fulton. Reprinted (2001).

Heard, D., & Barrett, M. (1977). Family learning In: *Irene Caspari, A Commemorative Symposium,* (collection of papers given at Tavistock Clinic memorial event).

Heimann, P. (1950). On counter-transference. *International Journal of Psychoanalysis, 31*: 81–84.

High, H. (1985). The use of indirect communication in educational therapy. *Journal of Educational Therapy, 1*(1): 3–18.

High, H. (1998). The potential space and indirect communication in educational therapy. In: *Feeling, Communicating and Thinking: Readings on the Emotional and Communicational Aspects of Learning* (pp. 161–193). Athens: Papazissis Publishers.

Hobson, P. (2007). *Cradle of Thought.* London: Pan Macmillan.

Hopkins, J. (2002) From baby games to let's pretend: The achievement of playing. In: B. Kahr (Ed.), *The Legacy of Winnicott: Essays on Infant and Child Mental Health* (pp. 91–99). London: Karnac.

Klein, M. (1931). A contribution to the theory of intellectual inhibition. *International Journal of Psychoanalysis, 12*: 206–218.

Klein, M. (1952). Some theoretical conclusions regarding the emotional life of the infant and our adult world and its roots in infancy. In: *Envy and Gratitude and Other Works, 1946 to 1963.* London: Hogarth, 1959.

Klein, M. (1963). *Envy and Gratitude and other works* (pp. 61–93). London: Hogarth

Klein, M. (1975). A contribution to the theory of intellectual inhibition. In: *Love, Guilt and Reparation and Other Works. Writings of Melanie Klein 1* (pp. 236–247). London: Hogarth Press.

Lewis, E., & Page A. (1978). Failure to mourn a stillbirth; an overlooked catastrophe. *British Journal of Medical Psychology*, 51(3): 237–241.

Main, M., & Solomon, J. (1986). Discovery of an insecure-disorganized/ disorientated attachment pattern: procedural findings and implications for classification of behaviour. In: C. M. Parkes & J. Stevenson-Hinde (Eds.), *The Place of Attachment in Human Behaviour* (pp. 95–124). Norwood, NJ: Ablex.

Main, M., & Weston, D. (1981). Quality of attachment to mother and to father: related to conflict behaviour and the readiness for establishing new relationships. *Child Development*, 52: 932–940.

Moore, M. S. (1990). Understanding children's drawings: developmental and emotional indicators in children's human figure drawings. *Journal of Educational Therapy*, 3(2), 35–47.

Morton, G. (2000a). Working with stories in groups. In: N. Barwick (Ed.), *Clinical Counselling in Schools* (pp. 142–158), London: Routledge.

Nagera, V. (1967). *Van Gogh: A Psychological Study.* International Univ. Press.

Osborne, E. (1989). Educational therapy: a personal overview. *The Journal of Educational Therapy*, 2(3): 1–17.

Perry, B. D, Pollard, R. A., & Blakley, T. L (1995). Childhood trauma, the neurobiology of adaptation and 'use-dependent' development of the brain: how 'states' become 'traits'. *Infant Mental Health Journal*, 16: 271–291.

Sacks, O. (2001). *Uncle Tungsten: Memories of a Chemical Boyhood.* London: Picador & Canada: Vintage, 2002.

Sletten Duve, A-M. (1988). The Norwegian educational assessment method. *Journal of Educational Therapy*, 2(1): 1–11.

Stern, D. (1985). *The Interpersonal World of the Infant.* New York: Basic Books & London: Karnac, 1998.

Strachey, J. (1930). Some unconscious factors in reading. *International Journal of Psychoanalysis*, 11: 322–331.

Van Gogh, V. (1979). *The Complete Letters of Vincent Van Gogh.* London: Thames & Hudson.

Winnicott, D. W. (1960). Ego distortion in terms of true and false self, quoted in Hopkins (2002), p. 93.

Winnicott, D. W. (1965). *The Maturational Processes and the Facilitating Environment* (pp. 140–152), London: Hogarth & London: Karnac, reprinted 1990.

Winnicott, D. W. (1971a). *Playing and Reality*. London: Tavistock & London: Penguin.

Winnicott, D. W. (1971b). *Therapeutic Consultations in Child Psychiatry*. London: Hogarth.

INDEX